﴿وَجَعَلَ بَيْنَكُم مَّوَدَّةً وَرَحْمَةً﴾

The Quest for Love & Mercy

Regulations for Marriage & Wedding in *Islām*

بِسْمِ اللَّهِ الرَّحْمَنِ الرَّحِيمِ

﴿وَمِنْ ءَايَـٰتِهِ أَنْ خَلَقَ لَكُم مِّنْ أَنفُسِكُمْ أَزْوَٰجًا لِّتَسْكُنُوٓا۟ إِلَيْهَا وَجَعَلَ بَيْنَكُم مَّوَدَّةً وَرَحْمَةً، إِنَّ فِى ذَٰلِكَ لَـَٔايَـٰتٍ لِّقَوْمٍ يَتَفَكَّرُونَ ۞﴾

الروم ٢١

« And among His signs is that He created for you, from yourselves, spouses that you may dwell (in joy and security) unto them, and He set between you love and mercy; surely in that are signs for those who reflect. »

[Ar-Rūm 30:21]

الآسرة المسلمة

The Muslim Family - 1

﴿وَجَعَلَ بَيْنَكُم مَّوَدَّةً وَرَحْمَةً﴾

THE QUEST FOR LOVE & MERCY

REGULATIONS FOR MARRIAGE & WEDDING IN *ISLĀM*

محمد الجبالي

MUḤAMMAD AL-JIBĀLĪ

مَنْشُورَاتُ ٱلْكِتَابِ وَٱلسُّنَّةِ

AL-KITĀB & AS-SUNNAH PUBLISHING

The Quest for Love & Mercy
Regulations for Marriage & Wedding in Islām
(The Muslim Family – 1)

28+183 p. 24 × 18 cm
ISBN 1-891229-51-6

Cover Design: ʿAbdullāh al-Jibālī

Printed by:
Al-Maktab al-Islāmī
P.O. Box 11/3771
Beirut, Lebanon
Tel: 961-5-456-280, Fax: 961-5-450-657

Published by:
Al-Kitaab & as-Sunnah Publishing
P.O. Box 2542
Arlington, Texas 76004
Tel. & Fax: 1-817-801-6933

TABLE OF CONTENTS

PRELUDE

Opening Sermon

إِنَّ ٱلْحَمْدَ لِلَّـٰهِ، نَحْمَدُهُ وَنَسْتَعِينُهُ وَنَسْتَغْفِرُهُ،
وَنَعُوذُ بِاللَّـٰهِ مِنْ شُرُورِ أَنْفُسِنَا وَمِنْ سَيِّئَاتِ أَعْمَالِنَا.
مَنْ يَهْدِهِ ٱللَّهُ فَلاَ مُضِلَّ لَهُ، وَمَنْ يُضْلِلْ فَلاَ هَادِيَ لَهُ.

Al-ḥamdu lillāh. Indeed, all praise is due to Allāh. We praise Him and seek His help and forgiveness. We seek refuge with Allāh from our souls' evils and our wrong doings. He whom Allāh guides, no one can misguide; and he whom He misguides, no one can guide.

وَأَشْهَدُ أَنْ لاَ إِلَـٰهَ إِلاَّ ٱللَّهُ، وَحْدَهُ لاَ شَرِيكَ لَهُ.
وَأَشْهَدُ أَنَّ مُحَمَّداً عَبْدُهُ وَرَسُولُهُ.

I bear witness that there is no (true) god except Allāh — alone without any partners. And I bear witness that Muḥammad (ﷺ) is His *ʿabd* (servant) and messenger. [1]

﴿يَا أَيُّهَا ٱلَّذِينَ آمَنُوا ٱتَّقُوا ٱللَّهَ حَقَّ تُقَاتِهِ،
وَلاَ تَمُوتُنَّ إِلاَّ وَأَنْتُم مُسْلِمُونَ۝﴾ آل عمران ١٠٢

---

1 The above two paragraphs, together with the following three portions of *Qurʾān*, are called *Khuṭbat ul-Ḥājah* (the Sermon of Need). Allāh's Messenger (ﷺ) often started his speeches with this sermon, and he was keen to teach it to his companions. The *ḥadīth*s in this regard are recorded by Muslim, Abū Dāwūd, an-Nasāʾī, and others, and are narrated by Ibn Masʿūd, Ibn ʿAbbās, and others (رضي الله عنهم). A full discussion of the various reports of this sermon is provided by al-Albānī in his booklet, "*Khuṭbat ul-Ḥājah*", published by al-Maktab ul-Islāmī, Beirut.

«O you who believe! Revere Allāh the right reverence, and do not die except as Muslims.» [1]

﴿يَا أَيُّهَا ٱلنَّاسُ ٱتَّقُوا رَبَّكُمُ ٱلَّذِي خَلَقَكُم مِّن نَّفْسٍ وَاحِدَةٍ، وَخَلَقَ مِنْهَا زَوْجَهَا، وَبَثَّ مِنْهُمَا رِجَالاً كَثِيرًا وَنِسَآءً، وَٱتَّقُواْ ٱللَّهَ ٱلَّذِي تَسَآءَلُونَ بِهِ وَٱلْأَرْحَامَ، إِنَّ ٱللَّهَ كَانَ عَلَيْكُمْ رَقِيبًا۝﴾ النساء ١

«O people! Revere your Lord who has created you from a single soul, created from it its mate, and dispersed from both of them many men and women. Revere Allāh through whom you demand things from one another, and (cherish the ties of) the wombs. Indeed, Allāh is ever-watchful over you.» [2]

﴿يَـٰٓأَيُّهَا ٱلَّذِينَ ءَامَنُواْ ٱتَّقُواْ ٱللَّهَ وَقُولُواْ قَوْلاً سَدِيدًا۝ يُصْلِحْ لَكُمْ أَعْمَـٰلَكُمْ، وَيَغْفِرْ لَكُمْ ذُنُوبَكُمْ، وَمَن يُطِعِ ٱللَّهَ وَرَسُولَهُ فَقَدْ فَازَ فَوْزًا عَظِيمًا۝﴾ الأحزاب ٧٠-٧١

«O you who believe! Revere Allāh and say just words. He will then rectify your deeds and forgive your sins. He who obeys Allāh and His Messenger has certainly achieved a great victory.» [3]

أَمَّا بَعْدُ، فَإِنَّ خَيْرَ ٱلْحَدِيثِ كِتَابُ ٱللَّهِ،

وَخَيْرَ الهَدْيِ هَدْيُ مُحَمَّدٍ (ﷺ)، وَشَرَّ الأُمُورِ مُحْدَثَاتُهَا،

وَكُلَّ مُحْدَثَةٍ بِدْعَةٌ، وَكُلَّ بِدْعَةٍ ضَلَالَةٌ، وَكُلَّ ضَلَالَةٍ فِي ٱلنَّارِ.

Verily, the best speech is Allāh's (ﷻ) speech; the best guidance is Muḥammad's (ﷺ) guidance; and the worst matters (in creed or worship) are those innovated (by the people), for every innovated

1 *Āl 'Imrān* 3:102.

2 *An-Nisā'* 4:1.

3 *Al-Aḥzāb* 33:70-71.

matter is a *bidʿah* (prohibited innovation), and every *bidʿah* is an act of misguidance that (whoever initiated it) will reside in the Fire. [1]

Defining Our Mission

Our goal in our works is propagating the true *Daʿwah* that derives from Allāh's (ﷻ) Book and His Messenger's (ﷺ) *Sunnah*. This is a duty that every Muslim should cherish. Allāh (ﷻ) says:

﴿وَلْتَكُن مِّنكُمْ أُمَّةٌ يَدْعُونَ إِلَى ٱلْخَيْرِ وَيَأْمُرُونَ بِٱلْمَعْرُوفِ وَيَنْهَوْنَ عَنِ ٱلْمُنكَرِ، وَأُوْلَـٰئِكَ هُمُ ٱلْمُفْلِحُونَ۝﴾ آل عمران ١٠٤

«Let there arise from you a group of people inviting to the good, enjoining the right and forbidding the wrong. Those will be the successful.» [2]

This *Daʿwah* has two fundamental aspects:

(a) *Taṣfiyah*: Cleansing and purifying the *Islām*ic beliefs and practices.

(b) *Tarbiyah*: Guiding and educating the people according to the purified teachings.

Allāh (ﷻ) indicates that this was the Prophet's (ﷺ) message:

﴿هُوَ ٱلَّذِي بَعَثَ فِي ٱلْأُمِّيِّـنَ رَسُولاً مِّنهُمْ، يَتْلُواْ عَلَيْهِمْ ءَايَـٰتِهِ وَيُزَكِّيهِمْ وَيُعَلِّمُهُمُ ٱلْكِتَـٰبَ وَٱلْحِكْمَةَ وَإِن كَانُواْ مِن قَبْلُ لَفِي ضَلَـٰلٍ مُّبِينٍ۝﴾ الجمعة ٢

«It is He who has sent among the unlettered a

---

1 Muslim and others have recorded from Jābir Bin ʿAbdillāh (رضي الله عنه) that Allāh's Messenger (ﷺ) used to start his speeches with this paragraph.

2 *Āl ʿImrān* 3:104.

Messenger from themselves reciting to them His *āyāt*, purifying them, and teaching them the Book and Wisdom — although they were before in clear deviation.» [1]

This is also an obligation on every Muslim according to his ability, as Allāh (ﷻ) commands:

﴿وَتَعَاوَنُواْ عَلَى ٱلْبِرِّ وَٱلتَّقْوَىٰ، وَلَا تَعَاوَنُواْ عَلَى ٱلإِثْمِ وَٱلْعُدْوَانِ﴾ المائدة ٢

«Help one another in righteousness and piety; and do not help one another in sinning and transgression.» [2]

Our mission is then to propagate the *Islām*ic teachings in various areas as follows:

1. Correcting Our Beliefs and Practices

We should revere, study, comprehend, and implement the noble *Qur'ān* and the Prophet's authentic *Sunnah* in accordance with the understanding and practice of the righteous *salaf*: the *ṣaḥābah* and their true followers, who are described in the following:

﴿وَٱلسَّـٰبِقُونَ ٱلأَوَّلُونَ مِنَ ٱلْمُهَـٰجِرِينَ وَٱلأَنصَارِ وَٱلَّذِينَ ٱتَّبَعُوهُم بِإِحْسَـٰنٍ رَضِيَ ٱللَّهُ عَنْهُمْ وَرَضُواْ عَنْهُ وَأَعَدَّ لَهُمْ جَنَّـٰتٍ تَجْرِي تَحْتَهَا ٱلأَنْهَارُ خَـٰلِدِينَ فِيهَا أَبَداً، ذَٰلِكَ ٱلْفَوْزُ ٱلْعَظِيمُ﴾ التوبة ١٠٠

«The first to embrace *Islām* among the *Muhājirūn* and the *Anṣār*, and also those who followed them in the best way — Allāh is pleased with them and they with Him. He has prepared for them gardens beneath which rivers flow: They will abide therein

1 *Al-Jumu'ah* 62:2.

2 *Al-Mā'idah* 5:2.

forever. This is the supreme success.» [1]

Thus, the guidance of the *salaf* is the only true guidance. Furthermore, the beliefs of the *ṣaḥābah* are the only acceptable beliefs:

﴿فَإِنْ آمَنُواْ بِمِثْلِ مَآ ءَامَنتُم بِهِۦ فَقَدِ ٱهْتَدَواْ﴾ البقرة ١٣٧

«So if they believe as you believe [2]**, they are indeed truly guided.»** [3]

Allāh warns against following any guidance other than the Messenger's (ﷺ) and his companions (ﷺ):

﴿وَمَن يُشَاقِقِ ٱلرَّسُولَ مِنۢ بَعْدِ مَا تَبَيَّنَ لَهُ ٱلْهُدَىٰ، وَيَتَّبِعْ غَيْرَ سَبِيلِ ٱلْمُؤْمِنِينَ، نُوَلِّهِۦ مَا تَوَلَّىٰ، وَنُصْلِهِۦ جَهَنَّمَ، وَسَآءَتْ مَصِيرًا﴾ النساء ١١٥

«Whoever opposes the Messenger, after guidance has become clear to him, and follows other than the way of the believers [4]**, We will give him what he has chosen and let him into Hell: What an evil destination!»** [5]

2. Inviting to the True *Dīn*

We should contribute to educating and guiding the Muslims to adopt the true *Dīn*, act according to its teachings, and adorn themselves with its virtues and ethics.

We should also contribute to inviting the non-Muslims to the unadulterated truth of *Islām*.

This is the only way for any person to attain Allāh's acceptance and

---

1 *At-Tawbah* 9:100.

2 The address here is to the *ṣaḥābah* (ﷺ).

3 *Al-Baqarah* 2:137.

4 The description "believers" here applies first and foremost to the *ṣaḥābah* (ﷺ).

5 *An-Nisā'* 4:115.

achieve happiness and glory. Allāh (ﷻ) says:

﴿وَٱلْعَصْرِ ۝ إِنَّ ٱلْإِنسَـٰنَ لَفِي خُسْرٍ ۝ إِلَّا ٱلَّذِينَ ءَامَنُوا۟ وَعَمِلُوا۟ ٱلصَّـٰلِحَـٰتِ وَتَوَاصَوْا۟ بِٱلْحَقِّ وَتَوَاصَوْا۟ بِٱلصَّبْرِ ۝﴾ العصر ١-٣

«By time, the human being is surely in loss, except for those who believe, do righteous deeds, enjoin upon one another the keeping to truth, and enjoin upon one another patience (in adversity).» [1]

3. Warning Against Deviant Beliefs and Practices

We should caution the Muslims and exhort them against any beliefs or practices alien to the pure teachings of *Islām*, such as *shirk* and *bidʿah*s.

4. Purifying the *Sunnah*

We should contribute to cleansing the *Sunnah* of weak and fabricated narrations. Wrong beliefs and practices deriving from weak reports have marred the beauty of *Islām* and prevented the Muslims' advancement.

The duty of purifying the *Sunnah* is so vital that the Messenger (ﷺ) praised those who perform it by saying:

«يحمل هذا العلم من كل خلف عدوله، ينفون عنه تحريفَ الغالين، وٱنتحالَ المبطلين، وتأويلَ الجاهلين.»

‹This knowledge will be carried by the trustworthy ones of every generation — they will expel from it the alterations made by those going beyond bounds, the false claims of the liars, and the false interpretations of the ignorant.› [2]

---

1 *Al-ʿAṣr* 103:1-3.

2 Recorded by Ibn ʿAdiyy, al-Khaṭīb al-Baghdādī, Ibn ʿAsākir, and others. It is reported from a number of *ṣaḥābah* including Abū Hurayrah, Ibn Masʿūd, and

5. Liberating the *Islāmic* Thought

Guided by the *Islām*ic principles, we should contribute to reviving the unobstructed *Islām*ic thought and opposing stubborn adherence to *ma<u>th</u>hab*s and prejudiced loyalty to parties. Neglecting this in the past has caused rust to dwell on the hearts and minds of Muslims, diverting them from the pure original sources of *Islām*, and causing them to deviate from the honest *Islām*ic brotherhood called to by Allāh (ﷻ):

﴿وَٱعْتَصِمُواْ بِحَبْلِ ٱللَّهِ جَمِيعًا وَلَا تَفَرَّقُواْ﴾ آل عمران ١٠٣

«And hold fast, all together, by the rope of Allāh, and be not divided among yourselves.» [1]

And by His Messenger (ﷺ):

«وكونوا، عبادَ اللّهِ، إخواناً»

‹Be, worshippers of Allāh, brothers.› [2]

6. Presenting the *Islāmic* Solution

We should contribute to providing realistic *Islām*ic solutions to contemporary problems, and strive toward resuming a true *Islām*ic way of life and establishing a true *Islām*ic society governed by Allāh's law. Allāh (ﷻ) says:

﴿وَأَنِ ٱحْكُم بَيْنَهُم بِمَا أَنزَلَ ٱللَّهُ وَلَا تَتَّبِعْ أَهْوَاءَهُمْ﴾ المائدة ٤٩

«Hence, judge between them in accordance with what Allāh has revealed, and do not follow their errant views.» [3]

Anas (ﷺ). All of its reports have various levels of weakness, but they add up collectively to make this *ḥadīth ḥasan*, as is indicated by al-Albānī in *Mishkāt ul-Maṣābīḥ* (no. 248), and as expressed by al-Ḥalabī in *al-Ḥiṭ ṭah* (p. 70).

1 *Āl ʿImrān* 3:103.

2 Recorded by al-Bukhārī and Muslim.

3 *Al-Māʾidah* 5:49.

We call upon all the Muslims to support us in carrying out this noble trust. This will surely elevate and honor them and spread the eternal message of *Islām* all over the earth, as is Allāh's true promise:

﴿هُوَ ٱلَّذِي أَرْسَلَ رَسُولَهُۥ بِٱلْهُدَىٰ وَدِينِ ٱلْحَقِّ لِيُظْهِرَهُۥ عَلَى ٱلدِّينِ كُلِّهِۦ وَلَوْ كَرِهَ ٱلْمُشْرِكُونَ۝﴾ الصف ٩

«It is He who has sent His Messenger with Guidance and the Religion of Truth, in order to make it prevail over all (false) religion, however hateful this may be to the pagans.» [1]

CONCLUSION

This work is, therefore, a humble response to our realization of a great responsibility: the responsibility to help bring forth before the English-speaking public writings that refine *Islām* and present it pure and simple, as close as possible to the way it was understood and practiced by its early righteous pioneers — the *salaf*.

Technicalities

TRANSLITERATION

We make a serious attempt to limit the use of transliterated Arabic terms to the following two situations:

a) There is no English expression that can reflect the same meaning as the original term.

b) The Arabic term is of such importance that it is essential to familiarize the readers with it.

At the end of this book, we have included a glossary defining

---

1 *Aṣ-Ṣaff* 61:9.

common Arabic terms that fulfill the above criteria. In addition, we have included an index of the Arabic terms that are more pertinent to this current work, indicating the page on which they have been defined.

Except for proper nouns, transliterated Arabic terms are *itali*cized. In general, the rules of English pronunciation can be applied. The following table includes additional symbols employed in this book to help pronounce the Arabic terms.

Symbol	Stands for	English Equivalent Sounds
ā, Ā	(ا) *Alif* (long vowel a)	Mostly: Man, sad. At times: Father, hard, god.
ū, Ū	(و) *Wāw* (long vowel u)	Root, soup, flute.
ī, Ī	(ي) *Yāʾ* (long vowel i)	Seed, lean, piece, receive.
ʾ	(ء) *Hamzah*	The first consonant vocal sound uttered when saying: at, it or oh.
Th, th	(ث) *Thāʾ*	Three, moth.
Ḥ, ḥ	(ح) *Ḥāʾ*	No equivalent. Produced in the lower throat, below "h". Resembles the sound produced after swallowing.
Kh, kh	(خ) *Khāʾ*	No equivalent. Produced in the back of the mouth and top of the throat.
Th, th	(ذ) *Thāl*	There, mother.
Ṣ, ṣ	(ص) *Ṣād*	A deeper "s" sound. Somewhat close to the "sc" in "muscle".
Ḍ, ḍ	(ض) *Ḍād*	Sounds deeper than a "d". Produced by touching the tongue to the mouth's roof.
Ṭ, ṭ	(ط) *Ṭah*	Similar but deeper than a "t".

Symbol	Stands for	English Equivalent Sounds
Ẓ, ẓ	(ظ) *Ẓah*	A deeper *thāl*, produced by touching the tip of the tongue to the back of the front teeth.
ʿ	(ع) *ʿAyn*	Produced in the bottom of the throat, underneath "ḥ".
Gh, gh	(غ) *Ghayn*	A gurgling sound produced in the back of the mouth, just above the *khā*. Similar to the "R" in some french accents.
Q, q	(ق) *Qāf*	Somewhat similar to the "c" in "coffee".

TRANSLATING AND REFERENCING *QURʾĀN* AND *ḤADĪTH*

The *Qurʾān* contains Allāh's exact words. These words cannot be exactly translated into other languages because of possible misinterpretations and limited human understanding. It is best to translate the meanings as understood by the Muslim scholars. This is what is attempted here. When an *āyah* is cited, the Arabic text is quoted first, followed, between double angle quotation marks («»), by the English meaning in **boldface**. The meaning is extracted from books of *tafsīr* and from accessible translations.

The location of a *Qurʾān*ic citation is specified in a footnote. It provides the name of the *sūrah* followed by its number and the number(s) of the *āyah*(s) cited.

Similarly, when we cite a *ḥadīth*, we provide the Arabic text for the Prophet's (ﷺ) words, and follow that by its meaning, in **boldface**, between single angle quotation marks (‹›).

A footnote normally specifies the location of a cited *ḥadīth* in the *Ḥadīth* compilations. The footnote indicates as well its degree of authenticity and the names of scholars who made such judgement. A *ḥadīth* narrated by al-Bukhārī or Muslim is automatically considered authentic.

NOTABLE UTTERANCES

Out of love, appreciation, gratitude and other noble feelings, a Muslim is encouraged to utter certain phrases at the mention of Allāh, His messengers, the angels, the *ṣaḥābah*, or other righteous Muslims. We present these phrases in condensed Arabic calligraphy as follows:

Phrase	Mentioned with	Transliteration	Meaning
سُبْحَانَهُ وَتَعَالَىٰ	Allāh's Name	*Subḥānahū wa taʿālā.*	He is exalted above weakness and indignity.
عَزَّ وَجَلَّ	Allāh's Name	*ʿAzza wa-jall.*	He is exalted and glorified.
جَلَّ جَلَالُهُ	Allāh's Name	*Jalla jalāluh.*	Exalted is His glory.
ﷺ	Muḥammad and other prophets	*Ṣalla 'Llāhu ʿalayhi wa sallam* [1].	May Allāh's peace and praise be on him.
عَلَيْهِ السَّلَامُ	Prophets and angels	*ʿAlayh is-Salām.*	Peace be on him.
رَضِيَ اللَّهُ عَنْهُ	A male companion	*Raḍiya 'Llāhu ʿanhu.*	May Allāh be pleased with him.
رَضِيَ اللَّهُ عَنْهَا	A female companion	*Raḍiya 'Llāhu ʿanhā.*	May Allāh be pleased with her.
رَضِيَ اللَّهُ عَنْهُمَا	Two companion	*Raḍiya 'Llāhu ʿanhumā.*	May Allāh be pleased with them.

1 Uttering this is sometimes described as, "saying *ṣalāh* upon the Messenger".

Phrase	Mentioned with	Transliteration	Meaning
رضي الله عنهم	More than two companions	*Raḍiya 'Llāhu ʿanhum.*	May Allāh be pleased with them.
رحمه الله	A past scholar or righteous Muslim.	*Raḥimahu 'Llāh.*	May Allāh have mercy on him.

When coming across any of these symbols, the reader is advised to utter the complete phrase in order to obtain the reward of saying the appropriate *thikr* or *duʿāʾ*.

PREFACE

This Series

Marriage is a subject of everyday's and everyone's concern. It plays a most central role in the human life, and has been largely discussed by the scholars of *Islām* through the ages, resulting in numerous writings. Some of those writings, especially by contemporary scholars, have been translated into English.

In the West, we find large numbers of people entering into *Islām*. With them, they often bring many misconceptions that they had inherited from their previous backgrounds, or that have been passed over to them from half-educated Muslims. A great deal of those misconceptions relate to marriage, divorce, and other family-related issues.

We find that most of *Islām*ic books on marriage are restricted in their scope, having been written for a different culture and background. They give little regard to problems and situations that concern the Muslims in the West.

This leaves quite a large gap that needs to be filled for the benefit of the Muslims in English-speaking countries, and this is what we attempt to fulfill in this 3-book series covering various aspects of marriage according to the authentic *Sunnah*:

1. ﴿وَجَعَلَ بَيْنَكُم مَّوَدَّةً وَرَحْمَةً﴾

" The Quest for Love & Mercy"

Fiqh of Marriage & Wedding in *Islām*

Covers the importance and advantages of marriage, selecting a spouse, the courting process, the marriage contract, marriage consummation, celebrating the wedding and the *walīmah*, and forbidden marriages; provides a practical procedure for performing the marriage contract; and includes a sample marriage certificate.

2. ﴿هُنَّ لِبَاسٌ لَكُمْ، وَأَنتُمْ لِبَاسٌ لَهُنَّ.﴾

"Closer than a Garment"

Marital Intimacy According to the Pure *Sunnah*

Covers the proper etiquettes of marital intimacy, forbidden acts of intimacy, the perils of *zinā*, and birth control; answers many frequently-asked questions about various acts of intimacy.

3. «رفقاً بالقوارير»

"The Fragile Vessels"

Rights and Obligations between the Spouses in *Islām*

Covers the obligations of the two spouses, the wife's rights, and the husband's rights; contains biographies of the Mothers of the Believers; paints very realistic pictures from the life of the Prophet (ﷺ) with his wives; and presents a complete discussion of the *ḥadīth* of Umm Zar'.

This series deals with marriage from a practical aspect, taking advantage of the author's many years of experience in the field of marriage and counselling. Each of its books serves as a handbook for performing marriage, learning the correct procedures for celebration a wedding, the "do's" and "don't's" of sexual life in *Islām*, and so on. At the same time, it maintains the soundness and precision in providing authentic evidence, which is customary in our books.

This Book

This is the first book in the marriage series. It deals with establishing a marriage — from beginning to end. This includes the importance and advantages of marriage, qualities to seek in a spouse, how to court a woman, conditions and requirements for the marriage contract, etiquettes for marriage consummation, wedding celebration, and forbidden women and marriages. It also point out a large number of violations to *Islām* that are commonly committed by Muslims at every step of the marriage process.

The discussion is simple and easy to follow. At the same time, it attempts to covers most of the issues that are usually dealt with under this subject. This makes it possible to use as a textbook in *Islām*ic colleges and institutes while, at the same time, keeping it easy to read and understand by the layman.

We make no claim to completeness in this book. The subject of marriage is extremely wide and very hard to encompass. We tried to include as many relevant authentic texts and explanation as was practically possible, but there surely are many additional issues that will need to be added in future editions — if Allāh so wills.

Finally, for our readers and ourselves, we make this supplication from the *Qur'ān*:

﴿رَبَّنَا هَبْ لَنَا مِنْ أَزْوَاجِنَا وَذُرِّيَّـٰتِنَا قُرَّةَ أَعْيُنٍ،
وَٱجْعَلْنَا لِلْمُتَّقِينَ إِمَامًا ۝﴾ الفرقان ٧٤

«Our Lord! Grant unto us wives and offspring who will be the comfort of our eyes, and make us leaders for the pious.» [1]

﴿رَبِّ ٱجْعَلْنِي مُقِيمَ ٱلصَّلَوٰةِ وَمِن ذُرِّيَّتِي، رَبَّنَا وَتَقَبَّلْ دُعَآءِ ۝
رَبَّنَا ٱغْفِرْ لِي وَلِوَٰلِدَيَّ وَلِلْمُؤْمِنِينَ يَوْمَ يَقُومُ ٱلْحِسَابُ ۝﴾

إبراهيم ٤٠-٤١

«My Lord! Let me establish the prayer, and the same for my progeny. Our Lord! Answer my *du'ā'*. Our Lord! forgive me and my parents and the believers on the Day of Reckoning.» [2]

Acknowledgements

All praise and thanks are due to our Lord (﷿) who facilitated completing this work. May He further reward all the Muslims who

1 *Al-Furqān* 25:74.

2 *Ibrāhīm* 14:40-41.

helped and supported this effort in various ways.

In particular, may Allāh (ﷻ) reward my *shaykh* and teacher, Muḥammad Nāṣir ud-Dīn al-Albānī (رحمه الله) whose works have benefited us in ways beyond description. May He also reward Sundus al-Asʿad who proof-read the manuscript, and ʿAbdullāh al-Jibālī who designed the cover.

We ask Allāh (ﷻ) to make this humble effort helpful and fruitful to the Muslims, forgive our shortcomings, purify our work from hypocrisy and conceit, and accept it from us.

Our Lord, forgive us and all of the believers, and bestow Your peace and praise upon our Prophet Muḥammad (ﷺ).

Muhammad al-Jibālī
27 *Rabīʿ ul-Awwal* 1421 H
29 June 2000

CHAPTER 1

A BLESSED BOND

Marriage Is One of Allāh's Laws

Allāh (ﷻ) created our world and the laws that govern it. Among Allāh's laws is that we need food to survive, air to breathe and revive our blood, rain to grow plants, and so on.

One of Allāh's important laws is that things are created in pairs. Those pairs must get together in certain ways in order for reproduction to occur. Allāh says:

﴿وَمِن كُلِّ شَيْءٍ خَلَقْنَا زَوْجَيْنِ لَعَلَّكُمْ تَذَكَّرُونَ ۝﴾ الذاريات ٤٩

«We have created all things in pairs, that perhaps you may remember.» [1]

This applies to human beings who are made of male-female pairs as well. Humankind started with our father Ādam and our mother Ḥawwā' (Eve). From that pair, Allāh (ﷻ) created all of the other people, as He (ﷻ) says:

﴿يَا أَيُّهَا ٱلنَّاسُ ٱتَّقُوا رَبَّكُمُ ٱلَّذِي خَلَقَكُمْ مِنْ نَفْسٍ وَاحِدَةٍ، وَخَلَقَ مِنْهَا زَوْجَهَا، وَبَثَّ مِنْهُمَا رِجَالاً كَثِيرًا وَنِسَآءً.﴾ النساء ١

«O people! Revere your Lord who has created you from a single soul, created from it its mate, and dispersed from both of them many men and women.» [2]

And He (ﷻ) says:

---

1 *Ath-Thāriyāt* 51:49.

2 *An-Nisā'* 4:1.

﴿يَـٰٓأَيُّهَا ٱلنَّاسُ إِنَّا خَلَقْنَـٰكُم مِّن ذَكَرٍ وَأُنثَىٰ، وَجَعَلْنَـٰكُمْ شُعُوبًا وَقَبَآئِلَ لِتَعَارَفُوٓاْ، إِنَّ أَكْرَمَكُمْ عِندَ ٱللَّهِ أَتْقَـٰكُمْ، إِنَّ ٱللَّهَ عَلِيمٌ خَبِيرٌ ۝﴾ الحجرات ١٣

«O people! We have created you from one male and one female, and have made you nations and tribes that you may know one another. The noblest among you in the sight of Allāh is the most pious. Verily, Allāh is All-Knowing and All-Aware.» [1]

This continues to be the way of reproduction for the humans, as Allāh (ﷻ) says:

﴿وَٱللَّهُ جَعَلَ لَكُم مِّنْ أَنفُسِكُمْ أَزْوَٰجًا، وَجَعَلَ لَكُم مِّنْ أَزْوَٰجِكُم بَنِينَ وَحَفَدَةً، وَرَزَقَكُم مِّنَ ٱلطَّيِّبَـٰتِ﴾ النحل ٧٢

«Allāh has given you spouses from yourselves, and has given you, from your spouses, children and grandchildren, and has provided you with good things for your sustenance.» [2]

Islām Urges the Muslims to Marry

Definition

The word commonly used in *Islām*ic texts for marriage is *nikāḥ*. In the original Arabic language, it means "intercourse". But it was then applied to the marriage agreement because it is a means to intercourse. [3]

Thus the statement, "He performed *nikāḥ* on the daughter of so and so," normally means that he executed an agreement for marriage. On

1 *Al-Ḥujurāt* 49:13.

2 *An-Naḥl* 16:72.

3 *Lisān ul-ʿArab*.

the other hand, the statement, "He performed *nikāḥ* on his wife," means intercourse. Mostly in this book, we will replace the word "*nikāḥ*" with its English equivalents to avoid confusion.

A Command from Allāh and His Messenger

Allāh (ﷻ) commands the believers to marry and help those under their charge to marry as well. He says:

﴿وَأَنكِحُوا۟ ٱلْأَيَـٰمَىٰ مِنكُمْ وَٱلصَّـٰلِحِينَ مِنْ عِبَادِكُمْ وَإِمَآئِكُمْ ۚ إِن يَكُونُوا۟ فُقَرَآءَ يُغْنِهِمُ ٱللَّهُ مِن فَضْلِهِۦ ۗ وَٱللَّهُ وَٰسِعٌ عَلِيمٌ ۝﴾ النور ٣٢

«Marry the unmarried among you and the righteous of your male and female slaves. If they should be poor, Allāh will enrich them from His favors. Allāh is Bountiful and Knowing.» [1]

Also, Allāh's Messenger (ﷺ) commanded the young people to marry, and advised those of them who could not afford it to fast as a means of controlling their sexual desire. Ibn Masʿūd (رضي الله عنه) reported, "We were with the Prophet (ﷺ) while we were young and had no wealth whatsoever. So Allāh's Messenger (ﷺ) said:

«يا معشر الشباب، من استطاع منكم الباءة فليتزوج، فإنه أغض للبصر وأحصن للفرج، ومن لم يستطع فعليه بالصوم، فإنه له وجاء.»

‹Young men, let him who can afford marriage marry, for it helps lower the gaze and guard the private parts (i.e. chastity); and let him who cannot afford it fast, for fasting is a repression (of desire) for him.›" [2]

Similarly, Anas (رضي الله عنه) reported that the Prophet (ﷺ) said:

---

1 *An-Nūr* 24:32.

2 Recorded by al-Bukhārī, Muslim, and others.

«عليكم بالباءة، فمن لم يستطع فعليه بالصومِ فإنه له وجاء.»

‹Get married. And whoever cannot afford it should fast, because it is a restraint (of desire) for him.› [1]

And ʿUthmān (ﷺ) reported that Allāh's Messenger (ﷺ) said:

«من كان منكم ذا طول فليتزوج، فإنه أغضٌّ للبصر وأحصن للفرج، ومن لا فالصومُ له وجاء.»

‹Anyone among you who has resources should get married, because it helps lower the (lustful) look and guard the private parts (i.e. chastity); and whoever does not (have wealth) should fast, because fasting is a restraint (of desire) for him.› [2]

ALLĀH'S PROMISED HELP

Allāh's Messenger (ﷺ) indicates that Allāh promises to help any person who aspires to marry in order to avoid sinning. Abū Hurayrah (ﷺ) reported that Allāh's Messenger (ﷺ) said:

«ثلاثةٌ حقٌّ على اللّه عونُهم: المجاهدُ في سبيل اللّه، والمكاتِبُ الذي يريد الأداء، والناكح الذي يريد العفاف.»

‹There are three individuals that it is a right upon Allāh to help them: a fighter for Allāh's cause, a *mukātib* [3] who wants to pay himself off, and one who seeks marriage for the purpose of preserving his chastity.› [4]

---

1 Recorded by aṭ-Ṭabarānī (in *al-Awṣaṭ*) and aḍ-Ḍiyāʾ ul-Maqdisī. Verified to be authentic by al-Albānī (*Ṣaḥīḥ ul-Jāmiʿ* no. 4058).

2 Recorded by an-Nasāʾī. Verified to be authentic by al-Albānī (*Ṣaḥīḥ ul-Jāmiʿ* no. 6498).

3 A slave who makes a contract with his master to purchase his freedom.

4 Recorded by Aḥmad, at-Tirmithī, an-Nasāʾī, and others. Verified to be *ḥasan*

In another report, Abū Hurayrah (ﷺ) said that Allāh's Messenger (ﷺ) said:

«حقٌّ على اللّهِ عونُ من نكحَ ٱلتِماسَ العفاف عما حرّم اللّه.»

‹It is a right upon Allāh to help one who seeks to marry for the purpose of avoiding what Allāh has prohibited.› [1]

Danger of Bachelorship

A strange phenomenon is occurring within the Islamic *Ummah*. It is not confined to one country or nationality. And its consequences, brought on by the Muslims themselves, can prove to have the most devastating effects on the Muslim community. This phenomenon is the alarming number of unmarried Muslim men and women.

On an individual level, it may appear that bachelorship poses a very insignificant threat to the *Islām*ic world. However in *Islām*, unlike other religions, matters are weighed in light of their benefits or harms to the community as a whole. So, what is the effect of single unmarried men and women on the community? To find the answer to this question, all one has to do is look at the non-Muslim communities. Every day we are confronted by the perversion and sinful ways that the *kuffār* find acceptable in their societies. This occurs because of their unnatural decision to abstain from marriage.

No Muslim in his right mind would want the Muslim *Ummah* to fall into lifestyles like those of Pompeii or Sodom and Gomorrah – towns that Allāh totally destroyed because of their perversion and disobedience. Protection against a fate similar to that can only be through lawful marriage.

---

by al-Albānī (*Ṣaḥīḥ ul-Jāmiʿ* no. 3050).

1 Recorded by Ibn ʿAdiyy. Verified to be *ḥasan* by al-Albānī (*Ṣaḥīḥ ul-Jāmiʿ* no. 3152).

Marriage Is a Practice of the Prophets

The Previous Prophets

The previous prophets of Allāh have married women, and none of them was known to be ascetic in regard to marriage. Allāh (ﷻ) says:

﴿وَلَقَدْ أَرْسَلْنَا رُسُلاً مِّن قَبْلِكَ وَجَعَلْنَا لَهُمْ أَزْوَاجًا وَذُرِّيَّةً ﴾ الرعد ٣٨

«And We have surely sent messengers before you (O Muḥammad) and granted them wives and offspring.» [1]

Our Prophet

The Prophet Muḥammad (ﷺ) indicated that marriage is part of his *Sunnah*, and that whoever neglects it is not of his true followers. Even though he derived the greatest pleasure and highest satisfaction from the prayer, Allāh's Messenger (ﷺ) expressed that he still had the desire for worldly pleasures such as women and perfume. This is only natural for a human messenger. Anas (رضي الله عنه) reported that Allāh's Messenger (ﷺ) said:

«حُبب إلي من دنياكم النساء والطيب، وجعلت قُرّة عيني في الصلاة.»

‹Of your worldly life, I have been made to desire women and perfume. But the satisfaction of my eye (or heart) has been made in the *ṣalāh*.› [2]

Marriage is the only permissible means of fulfilling the desire for women. 'Ā'ishah (رضي الله عنها) reported that Allāh's Messenger (ﷺ) said:

«النكاح سنتي، فمن لم يعمل بسنتي فليس مني. وتزوجوا

1 *Ar-Ra'd* 13:38.

2 Recorded by Aḥmad, an-Nasā'ī, and others. Verified to be authentic by al-Albānī (*Ṣaḥīḥ ul-Jāmi'* no. 3124).

فإني مكاثرٌ بكم الأمم يوم القيامة. ومن كان ذا طَوْلٍ فلينكح،

ومن لم يجد فعليه بالصوم، فإن الصوم له وجاء.»

‹Marriage is a *sunnah* (way) of mine; and whoever does not follow my *Sunnah* is not of my followers. Get married because I will display your outnumbering the other nations on the Day of Resurrection. Whoever has wealth should get married, and whoever does not should fast, because fasting is a restraint (of desire) for him.› [1]

Ibn 'Abbās (رضي الله عنه) said to Saʿīd Bin Jubayr (رحمه الله):

"Marry; indeed, the best of this *Ummah* (the Prophet ﷺ) had the most wives." [2]

NO MONASTICISM IN *ISLĀM*

Some of the followers of the earlier prophets tried monasticism as a self discipline that could possibly bring them closer to Allāh. However, they were not able to fulfill it as well as they had hoped. The reason is simply that it contradicts human nature, and that is why it is not permitted in *Islām*.

'Ā'ishah (رضي الله عنها) reported that Khuwaylah, daughter of Ḥakīm Bin Umayyah Bin Ḥārithah Bin al-Awqaṣ as-Sulamī (from the tribe of Sulam) visited her. Khuwaylah was married to 'Uthmān Bin Maẓ'ūn. Allāh's Messenger (ﷺ) saw her and noticed her messy appearance; so he asked 'Ā'ishah, «يا عائشة، ما أبذَّ هيئة خويلة؟» **‹O 'Ā'ishah! What makes Khuwaylah appear so messy?›** 'Ā'ishah (رضي الله عنها) replied, "O Allāh's Messenger! This woman's husband fasts during the day and prays during the night. So it is as if she does not have a husband, and thus she neglected her appearance." Allāh's Messenger (ﷺ) then summoned 'Uthmān Bin Maẓ'ūn and said to him,

---

1   Recorded by Ibn Mājah. Verified to be authentic by al-Albānī (*aṣ-Ṣaḥīḥah* no. 2383).

2   Recorded by al-Bukhārī and Aḥmad.

«يا عثمان، أرغبة عن سنتي؟» **‹O ʿUthmān! Are you doing that because you dislike my *Sunnah*?›** He replied, "By Allāh, no, O Allāh's Messenger! Rather, my whole interest is to follow your *Sunnah*." Allāh's Messenger (ﷺ) then said:

«فإني أنام وأصلي، وأصوم وأفطر، وأنكح النساء. فاتق اللّهَ يا عثمان، فإن لأهلك عليك حقاً، وإن لضيفك عليك حقاً، وإن لنفسك عليك حقاً. فصم وأفطر، وصلّ ونم.»

> **‹Verily, I sleep and pray, fast and break fast, and marry women. Thus fear and revere Allāh O ʿUthmān, because your family has a right upon you, your guests have a right upon you, and your self (body) has a right upon you. So, fast and break fast, and pray and sleep.›** [1]

In another report by ʿĀʾishah (رضي الله عنها), Allāh's Messenger (ﷺ) said to him:

«يا عثمان، إن الرهبانية لم تُكتب علينا، أفما لكَ فِيَّ أُسوة؟ فواللّهِ إني أخشاكم للّهِ، وأحفظُكم لحدوده.»

> **‹O ʿUthmān! Monasticism has not been enjoined upon us. Do you not have an example in me? By Allāh, verily I fear Allāh and safeguard His boundaries more than any of you.›** [2]

DISLIKING THE *SUNNAH*?

As we have seen above, fulfilling a natural desire in a lawful way is not wrong, and it does not represent a lack of piety. Rather, that is the

---

1 Recorded by Aḥmad and Abū Dāwūd. Verified to be authentic by al-Albānī (*Irwāʾ ul-Ghalīl* no. 2015).

2 Recorded by Ibn Ḥibbān, Aḥmad, and aṭ-Ṭabarānī (in *al-Kabīr*). Verified to be authentic by al-Albānī (*Irwāʾ ul-Ghalīl* no. 2015).

way of the Prophet (ﷺ) who is the most pious of all people.

To the same meaning, Anas (◉) reported that a number of men went to the houses of the Prophet's (ﷺ) wives and inquired about the Prophet's (ﷺ) manner of worship. When the Mothers of the Believers described that to them, they thought that he (ﷺ) did too little. Then they argued, "How could we reach Allāh's Messenger's (ﷺ) level, when all of his previous and later sins have been forgiven?" So one of them pledged, "I will always pray the whole night without sleeping." One said, "I will fast every single day." One said, "I will abstain from women and never marry." One said, "I will never sleep on a mattress." And one said, "I will never eat meat." When the Prophet (ﷺ) heard of that, he addressed them and others saying:

«أما والله إني لأخشاكم للّه وأتقاكم له، ولكني أصوم وأفطر،

وأصلي وأرقُد، وأتزوج النساء، فمن رغب عن سنتي فليس مني.»

‹Verily, by Allāh, I fear Allāh and revere Him better than any of you; yet I fast (some days) and break my fast (on others), I pray (part of the night) and sleep (the other part), and I marry women. So, anyone who dislikes my *Sunnah* (Way) is not (a follower) of me.› [1]

Advantages of Marriage for the Individuals

Being ordained by Allāh the Most Wise and All-Knowing, marriage is sure to have many virtues and advantages. In what follows we list a number of them.

1. PRESERVATION OF FAITH AND RELIGION

A righteous wife helps her husband preserve half of his religion. She provides him with help, support, and advice that help him obey Allāh and abstain from sinning. Anas (◉) reported that Allāh's

---

1   Recorded by al-Bukhārī, Muslim, and others.

Messenger (ﷺ) said:

«من رزقه الله امرأة صالحة فقد أعانه على شطر دينه،
فليتق اللّه في الشطر الباقي.»

‹When Allāh grants one a righteous wife, He has helped him (by that) to preserve half of his religion. Let him then fear and revere Allāh in regard to the other half.› [1]

In another report from Anas (رضي الله عنه), the Prophet (ﷺ) said:

«إذا تزوج العبدُ فقد استكمل نصفَ دينه، فليتق اللّهَ فيما بقي.»

‹When a servant (of Allāh) marries, He has (by that) completed half of his religion. Let him then fear and revere Allāh in regard to the other half.› [2]

Anas (رضي الله عنه) also reported that Allāh's Messenger (ﷺ) said:

«من تزوج فقد استكمل نصف الإيمان، فليتق اللّه في النصف الباقي.»

‹When a person marries, He has (by that) completed half of his faith. Let him then fear and revere Allāh in regard to the remaining half.› [3]

2. Preservation of Chastity

Men have a natural desire for women, and vice versa. Satan takes advantage of that to entice men and move their lusts when a woman approaches or moves away from them. He pictures her to them in an

---

1 Recorded by aṭ-Ṭabarānī and al-Ḥākim. Verified to be *ḥasan* by al-Albānī (*aṣ-Ṣaḥīḥah* no. 625).

2 Recorded by aṭ-Ṭabarānī (in *al-Awṣaṭ*) and others. Verified to be *ḥasan* by al-Albānī (*aṣ-Ṣaḥīḥah* no. 625 & *Ṣaḥīḥ ul-Jāmiʿ* no. 430).

3 Recorded by aṭ-Ṭabarānī in *al-Awṣaṭ*. Verified to be *ḥasan* by al-Albānī (*aṣ-Ṣaḥīḥah* no. 625 and *Ṣaḥīḥ ul-Jāmiʿ* no. 6148).

attractive and appealing form, which may lead them to various forms of sinning in compliance with their lusts.

Usāmah Bin Zayd (⚬) reported that Allāh's Messenger (⚬) said:

«ما تركت بعدي فتنةً أضرَّ على الرجال من النساء.»

‹I have not left after me a trial more harmful to men than women.› [1]

A married person has a quick means of protection against the Devil's whispers and seduction. Jābir (⚬) reported that the Messenger of Allāh (⚬) said:

«إن المرأة تقبل في صورة شيطان، وتدبر في صورة شيطان، فإذا أبصر أحدكم من امرأة ما يسره فليأت أهله، فإن عندها ما عندها، وإن ذلك يرد ما في نفسه.»

‹A woman approaches in the (tempting) form of a devil, and moves away in the (tempting) form of a devil. When any of you finds in a woman something that attracts him, he should go to his wife, because she has the same as the other woman has, and that satisfies his desire (in a lawful way).› [2]

3. ENJOYING LOVE, MERCY AND SECURITY

Love and mercy are important sentiments that brighten one's life and give him a feeling of reassurance, security, and happiness. One of Allāh's (⚬) great favors is the love and mercy that He instills among the married couple. They dwell into each other, just as one dwells into a house that gives him protection, security, and happiness. Allāh (⚬) says:

---

1   Recorded by al-Bukhārī, Muslim, and others.

2   This is a combined report recorded by Muslim, Abū Dāwūd, and others (aṣ-Ṣaḥīḥah no. 235).

﴿وَمِنْ ءَايَـٰتِهِۦٓ أَنْ خَلَقَ لَكُم مِّنْ أَنفُسِكُمْ أَزْوَٰجًا لِّتَسْكُنُوٓا۟ إِلَيْهَا وَجَعَلَ بَيْنَكُم مَّوَدَّةً وَرَحْمَةً ۚ إِنَّ فِى ذَٰلِكَ لَـَٔايَـٰتٍ لِّقَوْمٍ يَتَفَكَّرُونَ ۝﴾ الروم ٢١

«And among His signs is that He created for you, from yourselves, spouses that you may dwell (in joy and security) unto them, and He set between you love and mercy; surely in that are signs for those who reflect.» [1]

Furthermore, there is a wonderful feel of closeness between the married couple — similar to the closeness of a garment to a person's body. They provide for each other protection, comfort, and cover. Allāh (ﷻ) says:

﴿هُنَّ لِبَاسٌ لَّكُمْ، وَأَنتُمْ لِبَاسٌ لَّهُنَّ.﴾ البقرة ١٨٧

«They are a garment for you and you are a garment to them.» [2]

4. Lawful Fulfillment of Desire

As is indicated above, Allāh (ﷻ) has instilled in the human beings the desire for the opposite gender. This desire may be satisfied in unlawful ways that would have destructive effects on the individuals and societies — as is detailed later in this book.

Alternatively, one of Allāh's great favors on us is that he provided us with marriage as a lawful channel for venting our desires. Ibn ʿUmar and Ibn ʿAmr (ﷺ) reported that the Prophet (ﷺ) said:

«الدنيا كلها متاع، وخير متاع الدنيا المرأة الصالحة.»

‹This life is a temporary accommodation, and the

1 *Ar-Rūm* 30:21.

2 *Al-Baqarah* 2:187.

best of its accommodations is a righteous wife.› [1]

Ibn ʿAbbās (🙵) reported that a man came to the Prophet (🙵) and said, "We have an orphan girl under our custody. A poor man and a rich man have both courted her. She prefers the poor man, but we prefer the rich man. (What should we do?)" The Prophet (🙵) responded:

«لم يُرَ للمتحابَّيْنِ مثلُ النكاحِ.»

‹For those who like each other, nothing has proven as good as marriage.› [2]

5. PLEASURABLE WAY OF INCREASING THE GOOD DEEDS

Not only is marriage a lawful means of fulfilling a person's desire, but is also a means of increasing one's balance of good deeds.

Abū Tharr (🙵) reported that some of the companions of Allāh's Messenger (🙵) complained to him. "O Allāh's Messenger! The wealthy people have taken away all of the rewards. They pray as we do and fast as we do, and they give charities from their extra monies." He (🙵) replied:

«أوَليس قد جعلَ اللّهُ لكم ما تصَدَّقون؟ إن بكلّ تسبيحةٍ
صدقةً، وبكل تكبيرةٍ صدقةً، وبكل تهليلة صدقة، وبكل
تحميدةٍ صدقة، وإمرٌ بالمعروف صدقةٌ، ونهيٌ عن منكرٍ
صدقةٌ. وفي بُضع أحدِكم صدقةٌ.»

‹But has Allāh not given you that which you may offer as charity? Verily:
⇨ Every *tasbīḥ* (saying "*Subḥān Allāh* — Exalted be Allāh") is a charity;

---

1   Recorded by Muslim, Aḥmad, and an-Nasāʾī..

2   Recorded by Ibn Mājah, al-Ḥākim, and others. Verified to be authentic by al-Albānī (*aṣ-Ṣaḥīḥah* no. 624).

- ➪ **Every *takbīr* (saying "*Allāhu akbar* — Allāh is the Greatest") is a charity;**
- ➪ **Every *tahlīl* (saying "*Lā ilāha illallāh* — There is no true deity except Allāh") is a charity;**
- ➪ **Every *tahmīd* (saying "*Al-ḥamdu lillāh* — Praise be to Allāh") is a charity;**
- ➪ **Commanding good is a charity;**
- ➪ **Forbidding the evil is a charity;**
- ➪ **And having intercourse (with your wife) is a charity.›**

The companions asked, "O Allāh's Messenger! Would one of us fulfill his desire and yet get a reward for that?" He (ﷺ) responded:

«أرأيتُم لو وضعَها في حرامٍ، أكان عليه فيها وزر؟»

‹Assume that he directed it toward a prohibition (*zinā*), would that not result in a burden for him?›

They replied, "Yes, indeed." He (ﷺ) deduced:

«فكذلك إذا وضعها في الحلال كان له فيها أجر.»

‹Therefore, if he directs it toward that which is permissible (his wife), he gets a reward for it.›

Allāh's Messenger (ﷺ) then mentioned a number of other things that constitute charities, and concluded by saying:

«ويُجزِئُ من هذا كلّه ركعتا الضحى.»

‹And all of that may be covered by two *rakʿāt* that one would pray in the mid-morning.› [1]

Commenting on this, al-Albānī (رحمه الله) said:

"As-Suyūṭī said in *Ithkār ul-Athkār* that one's

1 Recorded by Muslim, Aḥmad, and others.

intercourse (with his wife) is a charity, even if he did not have any intention in that regard. My opinion is that this may be true for each intercourse, but he should have a prior intention in that regard at least when he first married her. And Allāh knows best."[1]

In a similar *ḥadīth*, Abū Tharr (ﷺ) reported that Allāh's Messenger (ﷺ) said:

«على كل نفس في كلِّ يومٍ طلعَتْ فيه الشمسُ صدقةٌ منهُ على نفسِه.»

‹It is required for every person, every day upon which the sun rises, to offer a charity for himself.›

Abū Tharr asked, "O Allāh's Messenger! How can I give charity when I have no money?" He (ﷺ) replied:

«لأنَّ من أبواب الصدقةِ التكبيرَ، وسبحانَ اللّهِ، والحمدَ للّهِ، ولا إلهَ إلا اللّهُ، وأستغفرُ اللّهَ، وتأمر بالمعروفِ، وتنهى عن المنكرِ، وتعزلُ الشوكةَ عن طريقِ الناسِ والعظمَةَ والحجَرَ، وتهدي الأعمى، وتُسمعُ الأصمَّ والأبكمَ حتى يفقهَ، وتدُلُّ المستدِلّ على حاجةٍ له قد علمتَ مكانها، وتسعى بشِدّةِ ساقيكَ إلى اللهفان المستغيث، وترفعُ بشدَّةِ ذراعيك مع الضعيف: كلُّ ذلك من أبواب الصدقةِ منكَ على نفسِك. ولك في جِماعِكَ زوجتَكَ أجرٌ.»

‹That is because among the forms of charity are:
- **⇨ *Takbīr* (saying "*Allāhu akbar* — Allāh is the Greatest");**
- **⇨ (Saying) "*Subḥān Allāh* — Exalted be Allāh";**
- **⇨ (Saying) "*Al-ḥamdu lillāh* — Praise be to Allāh";**
- **⇨ (Saying) "*Lā ilāha illallāh* — There is no true deity except Allāh";**

---

1 *Ādāb uz-Zifāf* p. 138.

- **(Saying) "*Astaghfir Ullāh* — I seek forgiveness from Allāh";**
- **Commanding good;**
- **Forbidding the evil;**
- **Removing thorns, bones, and rocks from the people's way;**
- **Guiding a blind man;**
- **Helping a deaf and dumb man hear and understand;**
- **Directing a person who lost something to his lost thing — if you know where it is;**
- **Running, with the power of your legs, to help one who is eagerly seeking help;**
- **Raising, with the power of your arms, an object for a weak person;**
- **Having intercourse with your wife: you get a reward for it as well —**

All of those are forms of charity that you give for yourself.›

Abū Tharr (ﷺ) asked, "How could I get a reward for fulfilling my desire?" The Prophet (ﷺ) responded:

«أرأيتَ لو كان لك ولدٌ فأدركَ ورجوتَ خيره فمات، أكُنتَ تحتسبُه؟»

‹If you had a child who reached puberty, and you expect good from him, but he died, would you seek Allāh's reward for that?›

Abū Tharr replied, "Yes!" The Prophet (ﷺ) asked: «فأنتَ خلقتَه؟» **‹Are you the one who created him?›** Abū Tharr replied, "No, it is Allāh who created him." The Prophet (ﷺ) asked: «فأنت هديتَه؟» **‹Are you the one who guided him?›** Abū Tharr replied, "No, it is Allāh who guided him!" The Prophet (ﷺ) asked: «فأنت ترزقُه؟» **‹Are you the One Who sustains him?›** Abū Tharr replied, "No, it is Allāh who would have sustained him!" The Prophet (ﷺ) then said:

«كذلك، فضعهُ في حلالهِ وجنّبهُ حرامَه، فإن شاء اللّهُ أحياه، وإن شاء أماتهُ، ولك أجرٌ.»

‹Thus, put him in what is lawful (intercourse with your wife), and avoid for him what is prohibited (*zinā*). Then, if Allāh wills, He would give him life; and if He wills, He would make him die, and you would be rewarded for that.› [1]

6. Living a Harmonious Life

Marriage allows a person to live in harmony with human nature upon which Allāh created the people. It would eliminate from him feelings of conflict and dejection. As indicated earlier, abstaining from marriage is an unnatural act that has been prohibited by the Prophet (ﷺ). To the same meaning, Saʿd Bin Abī Waqqāṣ and Samurah Bin Jundub (ﷺ) reported:

"نهى رسول الله عن التبتل."

"Allāh's Messenger (ﷺ) prohibited abstinence from marriage." [2]

7. Following the Way of the Prophets

We saw above that marriage is the way of the prophets. They are the individuals whom Allāh chose to be examples for the people. Their practices are all good, and it is our duty to follow them as much as we can.

8. Deserving Allāh's Help

We have cited earlier (p. 5) Abū Hurayrah's (ﷺ) *ḥadīth* in which Allāh's Messenger (ﷺ) indicated that Allāh (ﷻ) will surely help

1 Recorded by Aḥmad, Ibn Ḥibbān, and an-Nasāʾī. Verified to be authentic by al-Albānī (*aṣ-Ṣaḥīḥah* no. 575).

2 Recorded by al-Bukhārī, Muslim, and others.

anyone who marries intending by that to guard himself against sinning.

9. A LASTING RELATIONSHIP

When a married couple has a good relationship based on faith and *taqwā*, their relationship will extend into the next life and the woman will continue to be the wife of the last man to whom she was married in this life.

Abū ad-Dardā' (⌾) reported that Allāh's Messenger (⌾) said:

«أيما امرأة توفي عنها زوجها، فتزوجت بعده، فهي لآخر أزواجها.»

‹**Any woman whose husband dies and she marries after him, she will then be (in the hereafter) for the last one of her husbands.**› [1]

'Ā'ishah (⌾) reported that Allāh's Messenger (⌾) said:

«المرأةُ لآخرِ أزواجها.»

‹**A woman will be for the last one of her husbands.**› [2]

Social Advantages of Marriage

From the above discussion, we can conclude that marriage has many advantages to the society as a whole. In what follows we list a number of them.

1. PRESERVING HUMANKIND

Marriage fulfills Allāh's law for the reproduction, as we have discussed earlier. Thus it constitutes a correct means of preserving humankind —

---

1   Recorded by aṭ-Ṭabarānī (in *al-Kabīr*). Verified to be authentic by al-Albānī (*Ṣaḥīḥ ul-Jāmiʿ* no. 2704 & *aṣ-Ṣaḥīḥah* no. 1281).

2   Recorded by Ibn Khuzaymah, Ibn Ḥibbān, and others. Verified to be authentic by al-Albānī (*Ṣaḥīḥ ul-Jāmiʿ* no. 6691 & *aṣ-Ṣaḥīḥah* no. 1281).

until Allāh inherits the Earth and all what is on it.

2. Preserving Kinship Ties

Contrary to *zinā*, marriage preserves and reveres the kinship ties. It establishes the paternal relationships between the children and their parents, giving them all a feeling of dignity and self esteem. That strengthens the feelings of love and care within the society.

3. Safeguarding the Society from Moral Degeneracy

Marriage is the proper way to establishing correct and permissible relationships between men and women. This helps maintain chastity, and protects the Muslim individuals from slipping into the filth of *zinā* and other sins related to it (which will be fully discussed in a subsequent chapter). Thus, marriage closes the door in the face of many acts of moral degeneracy and decadence, which usually are among the major causes for the destruction of societies.

4. Safeguarding the Society from Physical Diseases

Together with *zinā* and its related vices come a host of destructive diseases. Among those are gonorrhea, syphilis, venereal ulcers, and, most recently, AIDS. Marriage is an important means of protecting the society from those and many other diseases that can be easily transmitted, and that do not spare even the children.

5. Establishing the Family Environment

Marriage is a necessary step for providing a healthy environment for nurturing and rearing the children. Our children are the fruits of our generation and the future men and women of our *Ummah*. Through good marriages, we furnish them with the love, mercy, compassion, guidance, and seriousness that they need for proper growth and development.

6. Increasing the Number of Muslims

Mere numbers do not count in the scale of *Shar*ʿ. But numbers of good Muslims are very important. They are the ones among the creation who elected to live by Allāh's (ﷻ) commands and follow His Messenger's (ﷺ) guidance. Such are the people who should increase and multiply so as to establish Allāh's religion in this life and enter His gardens in the next life.

A Muslim should marry with the intention of increasing the number of righteous Muslims. Subsequently, he should strive to raise his family upon to the true religion. Only then, would they be among the numbers of Muslims who will please and delight Allāh's Messenger (ﷺ) on Judgement Day to the extent that he will boast about them in front of the multitudes of nations who will then be present.

Abū Hurayrah (رضي الله عنه) reported that Allāh's Messenger (ﷺ) said:

«انكِحوا فإني مكاثرٌ بكم.»

‹Get married, because I will be exhibiting your large numbers (on Judgment Day).› [1]

Abū Umāmah (رضي الله عنه) reported that Allāh's Messenger (ﷺ) said:

«تزوجوا فإني مكاثر بكم الأمم، ولا تكونوا كرهبانية النصارى.»

‹Marry so that (on Judgment Day) I will be delighted by your outnumbering other nations. Do not practice monasticism like the Christians.› [2]

7. Strengthening the Muslim Community

When a nation multiplies in the right and lawful way through marriage,

1 Recorded by Ibn Mājah. Verified to be authentic by al-Albānī (*Ṣaḥīḥ ul-Jāmi*ʿ no. 1514).

2 Recorded by al-Bayhaqī and others. Verified to be authentic by al-Albānī (*Ṣaḥīḥ ul-Jāmi*ʿ no. 2941 & *aṣ-Ṣaḥīḥah* no. 1782).

it preserves the kinship relationships and protects its citizens from diseases, which results in a powerful nation. To the contrary, adultery loosens and severs the kinship ties, and results in the spread of diseases and perversions, which cause the nations to decline and fall. Allāh (سبحانه وتعالى) wants the Muslim *Ummah* to be a powerful nation capable of establishing His laws and spreading His guidance in a most efficient way. This may only be fulfilled through maintaining chastity with lawful marriage.

CHAPTER 2

SPOUSE SELECTION

In the previous chapter, we have established the great significance of marriage. With that in mind, a Muslim is urged to seek a partner that would help him attain the desired fruits of marriage in a most fulfilling way. This makes the task of selecting a spouse most crucial.

Selecting a Wife

A Conditional Choice

In *Islām*, a man is given some choice in regard to marriage. Allāh (ﷻ) says:

﴿وَإِنْ خِفْتُمْ أَلَّا تُقْسِطُوا۟ فِي ٱلْيَتَـٰمَىٰ فَٱنكِحُوا۟ مَا طَابَ لَكُم مِّنَ ٱلنِّسَآءِ مَثْنَىٰ وَثُلَـٰثَ وَرُبَـٰعَ، فَإِنْ خِفْتُمْ أَلَّا تَعْدِلُوا۟ فَوَاحِدَةً أَوْ مَا مَلَكَتْ أَيْمَـٰنُكُمْ. ذَٰلِكَ أَدْنَىٰٓ أَلَّا تَعُولُوا۟﴾ النساء ٣

«If you fear that you will not deal justly with the orphan girls, then marry whatever pleases you of (other) women: two or three or four. But if you fear that you will not be just (with them) then (marry) only one woman, or those that your right hands possess (of captives and slaves). That is better in preventing you from doing injustice.» [1]

However, "whatever pleases you of women" is a general directive that is further clarified in many texts of the *Qur'ān* and *Sunnah*. There are certain important qualities that a man should seek in the woman

---

1 *An-Nisā'* 4:3.

whom he wants to be his life-partner and the mother of his children. In what follows we mention the most important of those qualities.

1. RIGHTEOUSNESS

The first and foremost vital quality for a wife is righteousness. The Prophet (ﷺ) urged the men to seek a woman of faith and piety, and indicated that a man attains happiness through marrying her.

Abū Hurayrah (ﷺ) reported that the Messenger (ﷺ) said:

«تُنكح المرأة لأربع، لمالها ولحسبها ولجمالها ولدينها،

فاظفر بذات الدين، تربت يداك.»

‹A woman is sought in marriage for four reasons: wealth, social status, beauty, and *dīn*. So seek the one with *dīn* — may you then be successful [1].› [2]

Thawbān (ﷺ) reported that when the revelation came in regard to gold and silver [3], the *ṣaḥābah* (ﷺ) wondered, "What kind of wealth should we then keep?" And ʿUmar (ﷺ) said, "I will find the answer to that." He then rode his camel fast until he caught up with Allāh's Messenger (ﷺ), and he (Thawbān) was right behind him. He asked, "O Allāh's Messenger! What kind of wealth should we keep?" He (ﷺ) replied:

«ليتَّخِذْ أحَدُكم قلباً شاكراً، ولساناً ذاكراً،

وزوجةً مؤمنةً تعينه على أمر الآخرة.»

‹Let each of you keep a heart that is grateful (to Allāh), a tongue that remembers and mentions (Allāh), and a believing wife who would assist him in

1 Literally, the Prophet (ﷺ) said, **‹May your hands be filled with dust.›** This expression was common during the Prophet's (ﷺ) time, and it was not meant literally. It is an exclamation phrase reflecting encouragement or applause.

2 Recorded by al-Bukhārī, Muslim, and others.

3 *At-Tawbah* 9:34.

regard to the affairs of the hereafter.› [1]

A similar *ḥadīth* is reported by Abū Umāmah and ʿAlī (ﷺ):

«قلبٌ شاكرٌ، ولسانٌ ذاكرٌ، وزوجةٌ صالحةٌ تعينك

على أمر دنياك ودينك: خير ما اكتنزَ الناسُ.»

‹A heart that is grateful (to Allāh), a tongue that remembers and mentions (Allāh), and a righteous wife who would assist you in the affairs of your life and religion: those are the best treasures for the people.› [2]

The Wife Brings Happiness or Misery

A righteous wife is one of the main causes of happiness in this world. An evil wife, on the other hand, is a major cause of misery.

Saʿd Bin Abī Waqqāṣ (ﷺ) reported that Allāh's Messenger (ﷺ) said:

«أربعٌ من السعادة، وأربعٌ من الشقاء. فمن السعادة: المرأة

الصالحةُ، تراها فتُعجبُك، وتغيبُ عنها فتأمنُها على نفسها

ومالك؛ والدابّةُ تكون وطيئةً، فتُلحِقُك بأصحابك؛ والدارُ

تكون واسعةً كثيرة المرافِق؛ والجار الصالح. ومن الشقاء: المرأةُ

تراها فتسوؤك، وتحمِل لسانَها عليك، وإن غِبتَ عنها لم تأمنْها

على نفسِها ومالِك؛ والدابَّةُ تكون قطوفاً، فإن ضربتها أتعبتك،

---

1 Recorded by Aḥmad, at-Tirmiḏhī, and others. Verified to be authentic by al-Albānī (*aṣ-Ṣaḥīḥah* no. 2176).

2 Recorded by al-Bayhaqī (in *Shuʿab ul-Īmān*), at-Tirmiḏhī, Ibn ʿAbd ur-Razzāq (in *al-Muṣannaf*), and others. Verified to be authentic by al-Albānī (*Ṣaḥīḥ ul-Jāmiʿ* no. 4409).

وإن تركتَها لم تُلحِقْك بأصحابك؛ والدارُ تكون ضيقةً قليلة المرافق؛ والجار السوء.»

‹There are four sources of happiness and four sources of misery. Among the sources of happiness are:

(1) A good wife who pleases you when you look at her; and when you are away from her, you trust her in regard to herself and your property.
(2) An easy ride that enables you to catch up with your companions.
(3) A house that is spacious and of many facilities.
(4) A good neighbor.
And among the sources of misery are:
(1) An evil wife that viewing her dismays you, and who uses her tongue against you; and when you are away from her, you would not trust her in regard to herself or your property.
(2) A stubborn ride that if you whip it would tire you, and if you leave it alone you would not be able to catch up with your companions.
(3) A tight house of limited facilities.
(4) An evil neighbor.› [1]

2. Good Character

One should seek a wife who is known to be of good character or who has been raised in a good moral atmosphere. In a *ḥadīth* similar to the earlier one by Abū Hurayrah, Abū Saʿīd al-Khudrī (ﷺ) reported that

---

1 Recorded by al-Ḥākim. Verified to be *ḥasan* by al-Albānī (*aṣ-Ṣaḥīḥah* no. 1047 & *Ṣaḥīḥ ul-Jāmiʿ* no. 3056). The fourth item in this *ḥadīth* has been combined from another report recorded by Ibn Ḥibbān, al-Khaṭīb, and others, and verified to be authentic by al-Albānī (*aṣ-Ṣaḥīḥah* no. 282 & *Ṣaḥīḥ ul-Jāmiʿ* no. 887). A shorter form of this *ḥadīth* is recorded by aṭ-Ṭayālisī and verified to be *ḥasan* by al-Albānī (*aṣ-Ṣaḥīḥah* no. 1803 & *Ṣaḥīḥ ul-Jāmiʿ* no. 3629).

Allāh's Messenger (ﷺ) said:

«تُنكحُ المرأةُ على إحدى خصال ثلاثة: تُنكح المرأة على مالها، وتُنكحُ المرأةُ على جمالها، وتُنكح المرأةُ على دينِها. فخُذْ ذاتَ الدينِ والخُلق تربت يمينُك.»

‹A woman is (usually) married for one of three qualities: she is married for her wealth; she is married for her beauty; or she is married for her religion. So take the one of religion and manners — may your right hand then be prosperous.› [1]

A woman of low moral standards should be avoided, even if she had other attractive qualities such as wealth or beauty.

Abū Mūsā al-Ashʿarī (رضي الله عنه) reported that Allāh's Messenger (ﷺ) said:

«ثلاثةٌ يدعون اللّه عزّ وجلّ فلا يُستجاب لهم: رجلٌ كانت تحته امرأةٌ سيئةُ الخُلق فلم يطلّقها، ورجلٌ كان له على رجلٍ مالٌ فلم يُشْهِدْ عليه، ورجلٌ آتى سفيهاً ماله.»

‹There are three individuals that, when they supplicate to Allāh (عز وجل), their supplication is not answered: a man who has a woman of bad character and he does not divorce her, a man to whom another man owes money and he does not have witnesses over him, and a man who gives money to a weak-minded person.› [2]

In this *ḥadīth*, "bad character" pertains mostly to qualities such as

---

1 Recorded by Ibn Ḥibbān, Aḥmad, and al-Ḥākim. Verified to be authentic by al-Albānī (*aṣ-Ṣaḥīḥah* no. 307).

2 Recorded by al-Ḥākim, Abū Nuʿaym, and others. Verified to be authentic by al-Albānī (*Ṣaḥīḥ ul-Jāmiʿ* no. 3075 & *aṣ-Ṣaḥīḥah* no. 1805).

being loose and promiscuous in dealing with men, making the woman's conduct dubious and her chastity questionable. A man who keeps such a wife is a *dayyūth*. More on this will be discussed in the second book of this series [1].

3. Virginity

Virginity is not a condition for marriage, but is a recommended quality — provided that one has both options and that the women he is considering are equal in other respects. Virginity then becomes a weighing factor for a number of reasons that will be outlined in the subsequent sub-sections.

Jābir Bin ʿAbdillāh (ﷺ) reported that when his father died [2], he left behind nine girls that Jābir had to look after. Soon after that, Jābir married a non-virgin, and when the Prophet (ﷺ) met him he asked him, «تزوجتَ يا جابر؟» **‹Have you married, O Jābir?›** He replied, "Yes." He asked him, «بكراً أم ثيِّباً؟» **‹Is she virgin or non-virgin?›** He replied, "Non-virgin." He (ﷺ) then said:

«فهلاّ بكراً تلاعبها وتلاعبُك، وتضاحكها وتضاحكُك؟»

‹Shouldn't you have considered a virgin who plays with you and you with her, and she laughs with you and you with her?›

Jābir replied, "Indeed, my father ʿAbdullāh died leaving many daughters. I did not want to add to them another young girl like themselves, so I married a grown woman to take care of them and look after them." Allāh's Messenger (ﷺ) then said:

«فإنك نِعمَ ما رأيت، بارك اللّهُ لك خيراً.»

‹Indeed, you have made a good decision. May Allāh

---

1 See "Closer Than a Garment" by the author.

2 Jābir's father, ʿAbdullāh Bin ʿAmr Bin Ḥarām, was martyred in the battle of Uḥud. Jābir was then nineteen years old. Jābir lived ninety four years.

bless that tremendously for you.› [1]

4. Ability to Bear Children

Since one of the important purposes of marriage is reproduction, it is recommended to marry a younger woman who would normally be more likely to bear many children. In turn, this is more likely to apply to virgins than non-virgins.

'Abdullāh Bin Mas'ūd (ﷺ) reported that Allāh's Messenger (ﷺ) said:

«تزوجوا الأبكار، فإنهن أعذب أفواهاً، وأنتق أرحاماً، وأرضى باليسير.»

‹Marry virgins, because they have sweeter mouths (talk) and more fertile wombs, and are easier to be satisfied with little wealth.› [2]

Ma'qil Bin Yasār (ﷺ) reported that a man came to Allāh's Messenger (ﷺ) and said, "I have encountered a woman of honor and beauty, but she cannot bear children. Should I marry her?" He said, **‹No!›** After asking him two more times, Allāh's Messenger (ﷺ) said:

«تزوجوا الودود الولود، فإني مكاثر بكم.»

‹Marry the woman who is loving and can bear many children, because I will boast of your numbers (on the Day of Resurrection).› [3]

5. Loving Attitude

One should seek to marry a woman who is expected to have a loving and caring attitude toward her husband. This is normally possible to

---

1 Recorded by al-Bukhārī, Muslim, and others.

2 Recorded by aṭ-Ṭabarānī (in *al-Kbīr*). Verified to be *ḥasan* by al-Albānī (*aṣ-Ṣaḥīḥah* no. 623 and *Ṣaḥīḥ ul-Jāmi'* no. 2939).

3 Recorded by Abū Dāwūd and an-Nasā'ī. Verified to be authentic by al-Albānī (*Ṣaḥīḥ ul-Jāmi'* no. 2940 & *Irwā' ul-Ghalīl* no. 1784).

sense from the environment in which she lives and her family's reputation. This quality is indicated in the above *ḥadīth* of Maʿqil Bin Yasār (ؓ). Similarly, Abū U<u>th</u>aynah aṣ-Ṣadafī (ؓ) reported that Allāh's Messenger (ﷺ) said:

«خيرُ نسائكم الولود الودود، المُواسيةُ المُواتِية، إذا اتَّقَينَ اللّه.»

> **‹The best of your women are those who are bearers of many children, loving (to their husbands), comforting, and tolerant — provided that they have *taqwā* of Allāh.›** [1]

Ibn ʿAbbās (ؓ) reported that Allāh's Messenger (ﷺ) said:

«نساؤكم من أهل الجنة: الودودُ الولودُ العَؤود على زوجها»

> **‹Your women who will be of the people of *Jannah* are those who are loving (to their husbands), bearer of many children, and concerned (about their husbands).›** [2]

6. Contentment

An important quality to be sought in a wife is contentment. A dissatisfied wife would make her husband miserable and push him to do anything to please her.

It is easier for a virgin than a non-virgin to be content with her husband's financial situation and with what he gives her. Similar to Ibn Masʿūd's earlier *ḥadīth*, Jābir Bin ʿAbdillāh (ؓ) reported that Allāh's Messenger (ﷺ) said:

---

1 Recorded by al-Bayhaqī (in *as-Sunan*) and others. Verified to be authentic by al-Albānī (*Ṣaḥīḥ ul-Jāmiʿ* no. 3330 & *aṣ-Ṣaḥīḥah* no. 1849). The last part of it (about the crow) is also recorded by Aḥmad and others from ʿAmr Bin al-ʿĀṣ (ؓ) and verified to be authentic by al-Albānī (*aṣ-Ṣaḥīḥah* no. 1850).

2 Recorded by Tammām ar-Rāzī, Ibn ʿAsākir, and others. Verified to be *ḥasan* by al-Albānī (*aṣ-Ṣaḥīḥah* no. 287).

«عليكم بالأبكار، فإنهنّ أنتق أرحاماً، وأعذب أفواهاً،

وأقلّ خِبّاً، وأرضى باليسير.»

‹Seek (in marriage) virgins, because they have more fertile wombs, sweeter mouths, less slyness, and are easier to be satisfied with little (wealth).› [1]

And ʿUtbah Bin ʿUwaym Bin Sāʿidah al-Anṣārī (ﷺ) reported that the Prophet (ﷺ) said:

«عليكم بالأبكار، فإنهنّ أعذبُ أفواهاً، وأنتق أرحاماً،

وأرضى باليسير.»

‹Marry virgins! They have sweeter mouths, more fertile wombs, and are more satisfiable with little.› [2]

7. Naivety

Naivety, simplicity, and innocence of heart are commendable qualities to be sought in a wife, and are more present in virgins than non-virgins — because of their lesser experience in the ways of life. This is demonstrated in the above *ḥadīth* of Jābir (ﷺ).

8. Beauty

Beauty, wealth, and prestige are all mentioned the earlier *ḥadīth* of Abū Hurayrah (p. 24) as being secondary qualities that should not be sought at the cost of righteousness.

However, we cannot totally disregard these qualities — especially beauty. Abū Hurayrah (ﷺ) reported that the Messenger (ﷺ) said:

---

1 Recorded by aṭ-Ṭabarānī (in *al-Awsaṭ*) and aḍ-Diyāʾ ul-Maqdisī. Verified to be authentic by al-Albānī (*aṣ-Ṣaḥīḥah* no. 624 and *Ṣaḥīḥ ul-Jāmiʿ* no. 4053).

2 Recorded by Ibn Mājah and others from Sāʿidah and Jābir. It is verified to be *ḥasan* by al-Albānī (*aṣ-Ṣaḥīḥah* no. 623).

«خيرُ النساء التي تسُرُه إذا نظر، وتطيعه إذا أمرَ،

ولا تُخَالِفُه في نفسِها ولا مالِها بما يكره.»

‹The best of women is that who pleases him (i.e. her husband) when he looks at her, obeys him when he orders, and does not subject her person or money to what he dislikes.› [1]

Similarly, 'Abdullāh Bin Salām (🙂) reported that Allāh's Messenger (🙂) was asked, "Who are the best of women?" He replied:

«خير النساء من تسرك إذا أبصرت، وتطيعك إذا أمرتَ،

وتحفظ غيبتَكَ في نفسِها ومالِك.»

‹The best of women is that who pleases you when you look at her, obeys you when you order her, and safeguards you during your absence in regard to herself and your wealth.› [2]

A woman's appearance being "pleasing" to her husband applies first to pleasing him when he observes her righteousness and obedience to Allāh. But it may also apply to pleasing him with her physical beauty. That is why it has been ordained to look at a courted woman, as we discuss in the next chapter.

9. COMPATIBILITY

A man should seek a wife who is compatible with him, and a woman should seek a husband compatible with her. 'Ā'ishah (🙂) reported that Allāh's Messenger (🙂) said:

---

1   Recorded by Aḥmad, an-Nasā'ī, and al-Ḥākim. Verified to be authentic by al-Albānī (*Ṣaḥīḥ ul-Jāmi'* no. 3298 & *aṣ-Ṣaḥīḥah* no. 1838).

2   Recorded by aṭ-Ṭabarānī (in *al-Kabīr*) and others. Verified to be authentic by al-Albānī (*Ṣaḥīḥ ul-Jāmi'* no. 3299 & *aṣ-Ṣaḥīḥah* no. 1838).

«تخيروا لنُطَفِكم، فأَنكِحوا الأكفاءَ وأَنكِحوا إليهم.»

‹Make a (good) choice for your sperm (i.e. offspring): marry those who are compatible, and get married to them.› [1]

The question is in regard to the definition of compatibility. In general, it has two major requirements: *dīn* and character. These two qualities are among the required qualities for a wife that we discussed above, and are emphasized in Abū Hurayrah's *ḥadīth* in the next section regarding the husband.

Dīn and character may not be compromised and are the focal point for compatibility. A man or woman who is lacking in either of them is a poor candidate and should not be considered.

Other qualities may add to the compatibility between the two spouses, but none of them can be considered mandatory. Among the examples of compatibility factors is age, language, financial status, family status, national background, etc.

However, one must understand that, except for *dīn* and character, all of the other qualities are secondary and should not be overplayed, especially if they would be used as grounds for discrimination based on race, social status, country of origin, etc.

With the above understanding, we can say that age is an important "secondary" compatibility factor. It could become major if the age difference is such as to prevent one of the two spouses from being able to fulfill the marital rights of his (or her) partner.

Qualities Sought in a Good Husband

DĪN AND GOOD CHARACTER

The Prophet (ﷺ) instructed the guardians of women to marry them to men of good *dīn* and character. When a man of known righteousness and good character seeks to marry a woman, he should be seriously

1 Recorded by Ibn Mājah, al-Ḥākim, and others. Verified to be authentic by al-Albānī (*Ṣaḥīḥ ul-Jāmiʿ* no. 2928 & *aṣ-Ṣaḥīḥah* no. 1067).

considered.

Abū Hurayrah, Ibn ʿUmar, and Abū Ḥātim al-Muzanī (ﷺ) reported that the Prophet (ﷺ) said:

«إذا أتاكم من ترضون دينه وخلقه فزوجوه،

إنْ لا تفعلوا تكن فتنة في الأرض وفساد عريض.»

‹If one comes to you seeking marriage, and you are satisfied with his *dīn* and character, marry him; otherwise, a *fitnah* (harm) and great destruction will become rampant on the earth.› [1]

IS WEALTH IMPORTANT?

Unfortunately, when looking for a husband, the woman's family or *walī* first look at his bank account, instead of his *īmān, taqwā*, and *ʿaqīdah* (creed).

Furthermore, many Muslim women, whether living in *Islām*ic or Western countries, have been affected by the perverse ideologies of the West. They do not look for a man who possesses *taqwā* and character, which would guarantee for them a lasting loving relationship. Rather, they look for a man who has a strong buying power, owns a house, or possesses a higher degree of education — all at the cost of religion, morals, and, eventually, happiness.

Of course, we are not calling on all the Muslims to live in poverty; but we are emphasizing that wealth is a minor factor that should never be compared to *dīn* and manners. We should trust Allāh's (ﷻ) promise:

﴿وَأَنكِحُوا۟ ٱلْأَيَـٰمَىٰ مِنكُمْ وَٱلصَّـٰلِحِينَ مِنْ عِبَادِكُمْ وَإِمَآئِكُمْ ۚ إِن يَكُونُوا۟

فُقَرَآءَ يُغْنِهِمُ ٱللَّهُ مِن فَضْلِهِۦ ۗ وَٱللَّهُ وَٰسِعٌ عَلِيمٌ ۝﴾ النور ٣٢

«Marry the unmarried among you and the righteous of your male and female slaves. If they should be

1 Recorded by at-Tirmiṯẖī, Ibn Mājah, and others. Verified to be *ḥasan* by al-Albānī (*Ṣaḥīḥ ul-Jāmiʿ* no. 270 & *aṣ-Ṣaḥīḥah* no. 1022).

poor, Allāh will enrich them from His favors. Allāh is Bountiful and Knowing.» [1]

Whereas Allāh gives such a generous and true promise to the righteous, there is absolutely no guarantee that he will not, in the blink of an eye, take away the wealth of a man who is non-religious and ungrateful to Him.

No Comparison

When a woman marries a man possessing *dīn* and good character, she will not lose out in any respect: if he keeps her, he will do so in a good manner; and if he releases her, he will do so in a good manner. Furthermore, a man of *dīn* and good character will be a blessing for her and her children, and they will all help each other learn and improve in their *Dīn* and righteousness.

A woman should strongly avoid a man who does not have these attributes — especially if he is negligent of the prayers, drinks alcohol, commits *zinā*, or commits any of the other major sins. Wealth and social status should never be her main criteria in deciding for or against a husband.

Sahl Bin Sa'd as-Sā'idī (⁕) reported that once while the Prophet (⁕) was sitting with some of his companions, a man passed by them. The Prophet (⁕) asked one of the companions, «ما تقولون في هذا؟» ‹**What do you think of this man?**› Some of them said, "This is from among the noble people. By Allāh, if he seeks marriage, he deserves to be married; and if he intercedes, his intercession deserves to be granted." The Prophet (⁕) did not say anything. Another man then passed by them, and the Prophet (⁕) asked, «ما تقولون في هذا؟» ‹**What do you think of this man?**› Some of them said, "This is one of the poor Muslims. It is expected that if he seeks marriage, he will not be married; and if he intercedes, his intercession is not granted; and if he speaks, no one listens to him." Allāh's Messenger (⁕) then said:

---

1   *An-Nūr* 24:32.

«هذا خيرٌ من ملء الأرضِ من مثل هذا.»

‹This man is better than an earth-full of the likes of the other man!› [1]

1 Recorded by al-Bukhārī and Muslim.

CHAPTER 3

COURTING

Definitions and Examples

Definitions

When a man finds a woman of good attributes for marriage, his next step would be to propose to her or her family. We call this "courting" or "*khiṭbah*"; it is the act of asking for a woman's hand in marriage. Depending on the situation, the interested man may personally approach the woman or her representatives, or may ask some of his male or female relatives or friends to represent him in that.

If a man's proposal is accepted, the woman is considered "engaged" to him. This "engagement" counts as a legally unbinding attachment that precedes the full and binding attachment of the marriage contract.

Even though an approved *khiṭbah* is not legally binding upon the two involved parties, it still constitutes a mutual pledge for marriage; and breaking it without a valid reason would be an immoral act of dishonesty.

A valid reason for breaking a *khiṭbah* would be for the bride's side to discover a serious problem in the bridegroom of which they were not aware when they gave their approval. Similarly, if the bridegroom discovers a problem in the bride that he did not know when he asked for her hand, he may take that as grounds for breaking the *khiṭbah*.

Examples from the *Sunnah*

In a *ḥadīth* that will be fully cited in the next chapter, a man asked the Prophet (ﷺ) to marry a certain woman to him, and he (ﷺ) said:

«اذهب فقد أنكحتُكَها بما معك من القرآن.»

‹Go (have her as wife); I marry her to you for the
portion of *Qur'ān* that you have memorized.› [1]

In the case of 'Ā'ishah (⌾), who was a virgin, the Prophet (⌾)
proposed to her father. 'Urwah Bin az-Zubayr reported that Allāh's
Messenger (⌾) asked for 'Ā'ishah's (⌾) hand from her father Abū
Bakr. Abū Bakr (⌾) said, "But I am indeed your brother!" Allāh's
Messenger (⌾) replied:

«أنت أخي في دين اللّه وكتابه، وهي لي حلال.»

‹You are my brother in regard to Allāh's *Dīn* and
His Book. But as for her, she is permissible for me
(to marry).› [2]

On the other hand, the Prophet (⌾) approached Umm Salamah
directly. Umm Salamah (⌾) reported that when her *'iddah* [3] was over,
Abū Bakr proposed to her and she refused him. Allāh's Messenger (⌾)
then sent someone to ask for her hand on his behalf and she agreed. [4]

Abū Bakr Bin Ḥafṣ reported that when Ibn 'Umar (⌾) was asked
to propose on someone's behalf he would go to the woman's family
and say:

"الحمد للّه، وصلى اللّه على محمد . إن فلاناً خطب إليكم فلانة،

فإن أنكحتُموه فالحمد للّه، وإن رددتموه فسبحان اللّه . "

"All praise is due to Allāh, and may Allāh bestow His
ṣalāh upon Muḥammad. Indeed, so-and-so is asking for
the hand of so-and-so in marriage. If you marry her to

---

1   Recorded by al-Bukhārī, Muslim, and others.

2   Recorded by al-Bukhārī. Al-Albānī (⌾) indicated that, even though this is a
     report from 'Urwah who is a *tābi'ī*, he must have heard it from his aunt
     'Ā'ishah or his mother Asmā' (*Irwā'ul-Ghalīl* no. 1818).

3   A woman's waiting period after her divorce or her husband's death before she
     may remarry.

4   Recorded by an-Nasā'ī, Aḥmad, and others. Verified to be authentic by al-
     Albānī (*Irwā'ul-Ghalīl* no. 1819).

him, praise be to Allāh (for facilitating this); and if you reject him, exalted is Allāh (Who is above all deficiencies that exist in His creation)." [1]

Buraydah Bin al-Ḥaṣīb (ﷺ) reported that a group of *al-Anṣār* told ʿAlī (ﷺ), "Why don't you consider Fāṭimah (for marriage)?" Acting upon their advice, he went to the Prophet (ﷺ) who asked him, «ما حاجة أبن أبي طالب؟» **‹What does the son of Abū Ṭālib need?›** He replied, "O Allāh's Messenger! I came in regard to Fāṭimah the daughter of Allāh's Messenger." The Messenger (ﷺ) replied, «مرحبا وأهلا.» ***‹Marḥaban wa-ahlan*** **— Welcome, and a family member,›** and he said no more. ʿAlī went back to that group of *al-Anṣār* who were waiting for him. They asked him, "What do you bring?" He said, "I do not know, except that he said to me, '*marḥaban wa-ahlan*.'" They said, "Just one of these two words would suffice you from Allāh's Messenger (ﷺ); he offered you the 'family' and 'vastness'." [2]

A Common *Bidʿah*

A very widely spread practice among the Muslims of our time is that, when a man asks for a woman's hand and her family accepts his proposal, they all raise their hands and recite *al-Fātiḥah*. This practice is a *bidʿah* because it has no basis in the *Sunnah* or the practice of the *Salaf*.

Looking at the Courted Woman

Permission

When a man intends to marry a certain woman, and prior to formally

---

1 Recorded by al-Bayhaqī. Verified to be authentic by al-Albānī (*Irwāʾul-Ghalīl* no. 1822).

2 Recorded by Ibn Saʿd, aṭ-Ṭabarānī, and Ibn ʿAsākir. Verified to be *ḥasan* by al-Albānī (*Ādāb uz-Zifāf* pp. 173-174). A more complete version of this *ḥadīth* is cited in Chapter 5.

proposing to her, it is permissible for him to look at her and see as much of her as is normally possible. This would help him make the right decision and be sure that he truly likes her and would like her to be his wife.

Abū Hurayrah (ﷺ) reported that he was with the Prophet (ﷺ) when a man came to him and told him that he had just married a woman from the *Anṣar*. The Prophet (ﷺ) asked him, «أنظرتَ إليها؟» **‹Have you looked at her?›** He replied, "No!" He (ﷺ) said:

«أنظر إليها، فإن في أعين الأنصار شيء – يعني الصِّغَرَ.»

‹Look at her, because there is something in the eyes of the *Anṣār* — meaning smallness.› [1]

Al-Mughīrah Bin Shuʿbah and Anas Bin Mālik (ﷺ) reported that al-Mughīrah wanted to marry a woman, so Allāh's Messenger (ﷺ) said to him:

«اذهب فانظر إليها فإنه أحرى أن يُؤْدَم بينكما.»

‹Go look at her: it will then be more possible to have harmony between the two of you.›

He went to her house. She was inside her bedroom, and he met her parents and told them, "Allāh's Messenger (ﷺ) instructed me to look at her." They remained speechless, but the young woman raised one side of her bedroom's curtain and said, "I strongly reproach you! If Allāh's Messenger (ﷺ) instructed you to look at me, look. But if he did not, do not!" He looked at her, and then married her. He later mentioned, "No other woman attained her status (of love) with me, even though I have married more than seventy women!" [2]

Muḥammad Bin Maslamah (ﷺ) reported that Allāh's Messenger (ﷺ) said:

---

1 Recorded by Muslim, an-Nasāʾī, and others.

2 Recorded by Aḥmad, al-Ḥākim, and others. Verified to be authentic by al-Albānī (*aṣ-Ṣaḥīḥah* no. 96).

«إذا أُلقِيَ في قلب امرئٍ خِطبةَ امرأةٍ، فلا بأس أن ينظر إليها.»

‹When it comes into a person's heart to court a woman, it is permissible for him to look at her.› [1]

Also, Jābir Bin ʿAbdillāh (⁕) reported that he heard Allāh's Messenger (⁕) say:

«إذا خطب أحدكم المرأة، فإن استطاع أن ينظر منها إلى ما يدعوه إلى نكاحها فليفعل.»

‹When one of you courts a woman, if he could see of her as much as would convince him to marry her, he should do so.›

Implementing this instruction, Jābir (⁕) said:

"Afterwards, I wanted to marry a woman, so I used to hide to observe her — until I had seen that which led me to marrying her." [2]

CONDITIONS

When a man looks at a woman, that must be for the purpose of marrying her, and only if she is available for him to marry her. Looking for other reasons is a sin that must be avoided. Abū Ḥumayd as-Sāʿidī (⁕) reported that Allāh's Messenger (⁕) said:

«إذا خطب أحدكم المرأة، فلا جناح عليه أن ينظر إليها إذا كان إنما ينظر إليها لخطبتِهِ، وإن كانت لا تعلم.»

‹When one of you courts a woman, it is permissible

---

1   Recorded by Ibn Mājah, Aḥmad, and others. Verified to be authentic by al-Albānī (aṣ-Ṣaḥīḥah no. 98).

2   Recorded by Abū Dāwūd, Aḥmad, and others. Verified to be ḥasan by al-Albānī (aṣ-Ṣaḥīḥah no. 99 & Irwāʾul-Ghalīl no. 1791).

for him to look at her if he only looks because he seeks to marry her — even if she does not know (that he is watching her).› [1]

From this and other texts, we derive the following conditions for looking:

1. Looking should be for the purpose of marriage, and not for the purpose of fulfilling a desire or lust.

2. A man may only look at a woman who is available for him to marry, knowing that, should he propose, her family could possibly approve of him.

3. Looking should be without touching or *khulwah* (privately meeting with her).

4. Looking should be limited to the body parts that a woman is permitted to expose to strangers, namely, her face and hands. The difference between a casual look and the look of a man seeking marriage is that the latter is allowed to stare and repeat the look.

Some scholars, based on the above *ḥadīth* of Jābir (p. 41), permit the man to look at more than the minimum that we specified above. We do not favor this opinion for a number of reasons. Most importantly, it could easily be abused by the sick-hearted, opening for them a wide gate for defaming or lusting after innocent women.

If a man finds that looking was not sufficient in giving him a satisfactory idea about the woman that he intended to marry, he may send his mother, sister, or another woman from his relatives to look at her closely and tell him more about her.

Exchanging Photographs

With the wide availability of photography nowadays, a frequently

---

1 Recorded by Aḥmad and aṭ-Ṭabarānī (in *al-Kabīr*). Verified to be authentic by al-Albānī (*aṣ-Ṣaḥīḥah* no. 97).

asked question is whether it is allowed for the interested couple to exchange photographs.

Before answering this question, we need to point out a few important matters:

1. As we have indicated in various places of this book, photographs or pictures of beings with souls are generally prohibited in *Islām*. They are only allowed in situations of definite *maṣlaḥah* (benefit) for the Muslims, and when no other permissible means can fulfill the same purpose as they do.

2. If the photographs were determined to be permissible in a particular situation, they still need to fulfill certain criteria, such as not to show a prohibited thing, like a woman without full *ḥijāb*.

3. When a courter looks at a woman that he wishes to marry, his looking can be controlled by her or her *walī* so that it would not invade her privacy or exceed what is permissible. This is not the case with a photograph. A man can stare at it longer, show it to others who are not supposed to see it, and keep it in his possession even in the case where they have decided to terminate the courting negotiations. This leads to serious possible dangers — especially for the woman.

For all of the above, we believe that exchanging photographs is not permissible except in situations where one of the woman's *maḥram*s would show her photograph to the courter without leaving it in his possession.

Is a Woman Allowed to Look?

Just as a man is allowed to look at his intended wife, a woman is allowed to look at her intended husband — with the above conditions, and noting the a man's *ʿawrah* (prohibited parts) extend from his navel to his knees. Of course, a woman is expected to have modesty and shyness, and her looking should reflect that.

TALKING AND CORRESPONDENCE

Talking and correspondence are permissible between a man and a woman whom he is seriously considering for marriage. However, this should be done under controlled conditions: in the presence and watch of the woman's *walī* or his representative, avoiding *khulwah*, touching, or other prohibitions, and limiting it to what is necessary for helping the couple make their decision.

WOES OF INTERNET COURTING

The Internet is one of the newest and most powerful communication tools that were ever conceived by humanity. The average person nowadays spends many hours every week on the Internet: surfing, searching, reading, writing, learning, sinning, chatting, buying, selling, and so on. It is not surprising, then, that many individuals look for spouses in this wonderful land! Men and women "chat", e-mail one another, and even exchange digitized pictures!

However, our experience with courting and marrying over the Internet is very negative. We find that it involves many sinful or questionable practices, among which are the following:

1. Each individual paints about himself or herself a very unreal picture that is meant to impress the other side. One describes what he (or she) wishes to be, not what one really is! Being in a private room with a keyboard and a monitor provides a fat chance for pretence. Thus, lying and deceit are prevalent in this kind of communications. Asmā' (ﷺ) reported that the Prophet (ﷺ) said:

   «المتشبع بما لم يُعْطَ كلابسِ ثوبي زور.»

   ‹A person who pretends having that which he does not is like one who wears two garments of deception.› [1]

2. As we will see in the next chapter, a woman's *walī* is normally

1 Recorded by al-Bukhārī and Muslim.

responsible for investigating about a prospective husband's family, friends, manners, finances, etc. With Internet courting, on the other hand, a woman forsakes all of this and makes herself the ultimate judge, allowing her emotions and the courter's cunning make for her one of her lifetime's most important decisions!

3. A great deal of precious time is wasted in writing polished e-mails and exchanging worthless "chats". ʿAbdullāh Bin Masʿūd and Abū Burazah (ﷺ) reported that Allāh's Messenger (ﷺ) said:

«لا تزولُ قدما ابن آدم يوم القيامة من عند ربه حتى يُسأل عن خمس: عن عمره فيم أفناه، وعن شبابه (أو جسمه) فيم أبلاه، وعن ماله من أين اكتسبه وفيم أنفقه، وماذا عمل فيما علم؟»

‹A human being's feet will not depart from before his Lord, on the Day of Resurrection, until he is questioned about five things: his lifetime and how he consumed it, his youth and body and how he utilized it, his wealth and how he earn it and how he spend it, and what he did in regard to what he knew› [1]

4. Digitized pictures are often exchanged. As indicated above, this practice is largely prohibited, especially since digitized pictures can be easily and permanently stored on the computer, and electronically exchanged with other "interested" individuals.

5. In many cases, the Internet communication takes place between a man and a married woman (often with children)! Soon, the woman starts seeing her husband's mistakes well magnified, and her Internet chatter grows in her thoughts into a perfect hero that will surely save her from her miserable life with her husband. We have witnessed a number of such cases that ended in divorce, or in the woman running away from her husband's house to join the hero that she never met! As we will see in the next section, turning a

---

1 Recorded by at-Tirmithī. Verified to be authentic by al-Albānī (*aṣ-Ṣaḥīḥah* no. 946).

woman against her husband is a great sin.

Because of the above and many other reasons, we see that Internet courting is a dangerous practice that should be totally avoided by the righteous Muslims.

It is interesting to note that, in many cases of Internet courting and marriage that the author came to handle, not even one case ended in a happy marriage and was clear of violations to *Islām*!

Prohibited Courting

Courting a Married Woman

It is prohibited to court a woman who is married. The same is true about a woman whose husband divorced her a non-final divorce (a first or second time) and she is still in her *ʿiddah* (waiting period). The reason for this is that in both cases she is considered under the authority of her husband, and no other man may challenge that authority.

It is indeed a great sin to turn a woman against her husband with the intention of marrying her. Abū Hurayrah and Buraydah (ﷺ) reported that Allāh's Messenger (ﷺ) said:

«ليس منا من خبّب امرأةً على زوجها، أو عبداً على سيده.»

‹He is not one of us who turns a woman against her husband or a slave against his master.› [1]

Courting a Woman Who is Being Courted

When a Muslim man is proposing to a woman, it is not permissible for other Muslims to propose to her. They should wait until her side (she, her family, or her representative) takes a clear position from the

1 Recorded by Abū Dāwūd, Aḥmad, al-Ḥākim, and others. Verified to be authentic by al-Albānī (*Ṣaḥīḥ ul-Jāmiʿ* no. 5436, 5437, 6223, & *aṣ-Ṣaḥīḥah* no. 324, 325).

proposal: either acceptance or rejection. If that proposal is rejected, others may then approach her for marriage.

Abū Hurayrah (﷡) reported that Allāh's Messenger (ﷺ) said:

«إياكم والظَّنَّ، فإن الظن أكذب الحديث، ولا تجسّسوا، ولا تحسَّسوا، ولا تنافسوا، ولا تحاسدوا، ولا تباغضوا، ولا تدابروا، وكونوا عباد اللَّهِ إخوائًا، ولا يخطب الرجل على خطبة أخيه حتى ينكح أو يترك. »

‹Avoid suspicion, for suspicion is the worst of false tales. Do not spy, do not look for the faults (of each other), do not oppose each other, do not envy one another, do no hate one another, do not desert each other — and, O Servants of Allāh, be (true) brothers. Let not a man court a woman whom his brother is courting: (He should wait) until he marries or leaves her.› [1]

'Uqbah Bin 'Āmir (﷡) reported that Allāh's Messenger (ﷺ) said:

«المؤمن أخو المؤمن، فلا يحل للمؤمن أن يبتاع على بيع أخيه، ولا يخطبَ على خِطبة إخيه، حتى يذر. »

‹A believer is a brother to another believer. It is not permissible for a believer to negotiate a deal that his brother is negotiating, nor propose to a woman to whom his brother is proposing — until he leaves.› [2]

Abū Hurayrah (﷡) reported that Allāh's Messenger (ﷺ) said:

«لا يخطب أحدُكم على خِطبة أخيه، حتى ينكح أو يترُك. »

‹Let not any of you propose to a woman to whom his brother is proposing. (He should wait) until he

---

1   Recorded by al-Bukhārī, Muslim, and others.
2   Recorded by Muslim.

marries or quits.› [1]

'Abdullāh Bin 'Umar (ﷺ) reported that Allāh's Messenger (ﷺ) said:

«لا يبع بعضكم على بيع بعض، ولا يَخْطِب بعضُكم على خِطبة بعض.»

‹Let none of you negotiate a deal that is being negotiated by another one, nor propose to a woman to whom another one is proposing.› [2]

Abū Hurayrah (ﷺ) reported that Allāh's Messenger (ﷺ) said:

«لا يَخْطِبُ الرجل على خِطبةِ أخيه، ولا يسومُ على سوم أخيه، ولا تُنكحُ المرأة على عمتها ولا على خالتها، ولا تَسأَلُ المرأةُ طلاق أختها لتَكفئَ صَحْفَتَها ولتُنكحَ، فإنما لها ما كتب اللّهُ لها.»

‹Let not a man propose to a woman to whom his brother is proposing, nor negotiate a deal that his brother is negotiating. A woman may not be married to a man who is married to her paternal or maternal aunt. A woman should not request that her sister be divorced so that she would fill her own plate (with food) or get married (instead of her), because she will only receive what Allāh has prescribed for her.› [3]

Other Prohibited Forms

The following forms of courting are also prohibited:

1. A man who has four wives may not court an additional

---

1 Recorded by an-Nasā'ī. Verified to be authentic by al-Albānī (*Irwā' ul-Ghalīl* no. 1817 & *aṣ-Ṣaḥīḥah* no. 1030).

2 Recorded by al-Bukhārī, an-Nasā'ī, and others.

3 Recorded by Muslim.

woman — unless he divorces one or more of his wives.

2. A man is not allowed to court a woman whom he is not allowed to simultaneously marry with a current wife, such as her sister or aunt.

3. A man who had divorced a wife three times is not allowed to court or consider her unless she married after him another man who, after consummating their marriage, willfully divorces her.

4. A woman who is in her *'iddah* from a husband's death or a terminal divorce [1] may not be approached with direct proposals. She may only be approached indirectly — until her *'iddah* is over. Allāh (ﷻ) says:

﴿وَلَا جُنَاحَ عَلَيْكُمْ فِيمَا عَرَّضْتُم بِهِ مِنْ خِطْبَةِ ٱلنِّسَآءِ أَوْ أَكْنَنتُمْ فِيٓ أَنفُسِكُمْ؛ عَلِمَ ٱللَّهُ أَنَّكُمْ سَتَذْكُرُونَهُنَّ، وَلَٰكِن لَّا تُوَاعِدُوهُنَّ سِرًّا إِلَّآ أَن تَقُولُوا۟ قَوْلًا مَّعْرُوفًا؛ وَلَا تَعْزِمُوا۟ عُقْدَةَ ٱلنِّكَاحِ حَتَّىٰ يَبْلُغَ ٱلْكِتَٰبُ أَجَلَهُۥ. وَٱعْلَمُوٓا۟ أَنَّ ٱللَّهَ يَعْلَمُ مَا فِيٓ أَنفُسِكُمْ فَٱحْذَرُوهُ، وَٱعْلَمُوٓا۟ أَنَّ ٱللَّهَ غَفُورٌ حَلِيمٌ ۝﴾ البقرة ٢٣٥

«There is no blame upon you for that to which you (indirectly) allude concerning a proposal to women, nor for what you conceal within yourselves. Allāh knows that you are going to remember them. But do not promise them secretly except for saying a proper saying. And do not decide to undertake a marriage contract until the decreed period reaches its end. And know that Allāh knows what is within yourselves, so beware of Him. And know that Allāh is Forgiving and Tolerant.»

---

1 This includes a third and final divorce, or marriage termination through *khul'* (upon her request) or *faskh* (by the judge's decree).

Offering a Woman for Marriage

It is permissible for a man to offer his daughter or principal for marriage to those whom he trusts as being worthy of her.

ʿAbdullāh Bin ʿUmar (ﷺ) reported that after the death of his sister Ḥafṣah's husband, Khunays Bin Ḥuthāfah as-Sahmī (ﷺ), ʿUmar (ﷺ) offered Ḥafṣah (ﷺ) to ʿUthmān (ﷺ). A few nights later, ʿUthmān apologized, "I have decided not to marry right now." ʿUmar then offered her to Abū Bakr (ﷺ), and he did not give him an answer either. That saddened ʿUmar; but the Prophet (ﷺ) consoled him saying:

«يتزوج حفصةَ من هو خير عثمانَ،

ويتزوج عثمانُ من هي خير من حفصة.»

‹One who is better than ʿUthmān will marry Ḥafṣah, and ʿUthmān will marry one who is better than Ḥafṣah.› [1]

A few nights later, Allāh's Messenger (ﷺ) asked him for her hand, and ʿUmar accepted. Later on, Abū Bakr met ʿUmar and asked him, "You were probably bothered when you offered me Ḥafṣah and I did not give you an answer." ʿUmar said, "Yes!" Abū Bakr (ﷺ) then explained:

> "Truly, what had prevented me from giving you an answer when you offered her to me was that I knew that Allāh's Messenger (ﷺ) had mentioned (marrying) her, and I was not to expose Allāh's Messenger's (ﷺ) secret. Had he relinquished her, I would surely have accepted her." [2]

Allāh (ﷻ) tells us about another case where a righteous man offered one of his two daughters in marriage to Mūsā (ﷺ):

1 Recorded by al-Bukhārī and Ibn Saʿd.

2 Recorded by al-Bukhārī, an-Nasāʾī, and others.

﴿قال إنّي أُريدُ أَنْ أُنكِحَكَ إحْدَى ٱبْنَتَيَّ هَـٰتَيْنِ عَلَىٰ أَن تَأْجُرَنِي ثَمَـٰنِيَ حِجَجٍ، فَإِنْ أَتْمَمْتَ عَشْرًا فَمِنْ عِندِكَ﴾ القصص ٢٧

«He said, "Indeed, I wish to marry to you one of these two daughters of mine, on condition that you serve me for (at least) eight years; but if you complete ten, it will be (a favor) from you."» [1]

Performing *Istikhārah* and Seeking Advice

DESCRIPTION OF *ISTIKHĀRAH*

Istikhārah means seeking the good through relinquishing one's choice to Allāh. A believer should perform *istikhārah* before starting any important undertaking. Since marriage is one of the most important decisions that a person takes, it is important for both the man and woman to perform *istikhārah* before they give the final word that binds them together.

Jābir Bin ʿAbdillāh (ﷺ) reported that Allāh's Messenger (ﷺ) used to teach his companions to perform *istikhārah* in all of their affairs — like teaching them a *sūrah* from the *Qurʾān*. He told them:

«إذا هم أحدُكم بالأمر، فليركع ركعتين من غير الفريضةِ، ثم ليقُل: "اللّـٰهم إني أستخيرُك بعلمِك، وأستقدِرُك بقُدرتِك، وأسألُكَ من فضلِك العظيمِ، فإنّك تقدِرُ ولا أقدِرُ، وتَعلمُ ولا أعلمُ، وأنت علامُ الغُيوبِ. اللّـٰهم إن كُنتَ تعلمُ أن هذا الأمرَ (وتُسميه بٱسمه) هو خيرٌ لي في ديني ومعاشي، وعاقبةِ أمري وعاجِلِه وآجِلِه، فٱقْدُرهُ لي، ويَسِّره لي، ثم بارِكْ لي فيه. وإن كُنتَ تعلمُ أن هذا الأمرَ شرٌّ لي في ديني ومعاشي، وعاقبةِ أمري وعاجِلِه وآجِلِه، فٱصرِفهُ عني،

1 *Al-Qaṣaṣ* 28:27.

واْصرفني عنه، واْقدُرْ ليَ الخيرَ حيثُ كانَ، ثمّ رَضِّني به." وما
ندِم من اْستخار الخالقَ، وشاور المخلوقين، وتثبّتَ في أمره.»

‹When one of you is about to do something (important), let him pray two non-obligatory *rakʿāt* and then say:
"*Allāhumma innī astakhīruka bi-ʿilmika, wa-astaqdiruka bi-qudratika, wa-asʾaluka min faḍlik al-aẓīm, fa-ʾinnaka taqdiru wa-lā aqdir, wa-taʿlamu wa-lā aʿlam, wa-ʾanta ʿallām ul-ghuyūb. Allāhumma in kunta taʿlamu anna hātha ʾl-ʾamra* (and he names his intended affair) *huwa khayrun lī fī dīnī wa-maʿāshī, wa-ʿāqibati amrī wa-ʿājilihī wa-ʾājilihī, fa-qdurhu lī, wa-yassirhu lī, thumma bārik lī fīh. Wa-in kunta taʿlamu anna hātha ʾl-ʾamra huwa sharrun lī fī dīnī wa-maʿāshī, wa-ʿāqibati amrī wa-ʿājilihī wa-ʾājilihī, fa-ṣrifhu ʿannī wa-ṣrifnī ʿanhu, wa-qdur liy-al-khayra ḥaythu kān, thumma raḍḍinī bih* —
O Allāh, I ask You to choose for me with Your knowledge and decree from me with Your might, and I ask You of Your great favor. Indeed, You decree and I do not, and You know and I do not; You surely are the Knower of all that is hidden. O Allāh, if You know that this affair (and he names it) is good for me in regard to my religion, my living, and its outcome — both immediate and postponed, then decree it for me, facilitate it for me, and then bless it for me. And if You know that this affair is harmful for me in regard to my religion, my living, and its outcome — both immediate and postponed, then divert it from me and divert me from it, and decree for me the good wherever it may be, and then make me content by it."

And indeed, never would he regret who asks the Creator to choose for him, and consults with the

creation, and ascertains his actions.› [1]

MISCONCEPTIONS ABOUT *ISTIKHĀRAH*

Some people think that one of the important requirements of *istikhārah* is that it be performed before going to sleep, and that one should see some dreams telling him what to do. Others think that, as a result of the *istikhārah*, one should feel in his heart an inclination toward the proper choice.

There is no basis for either of the above two assumptions, and the above *ḥadīth* supports neither. In fact, the *ḥadīth* indicates that when, as a result of the *istikhārah*, Allāh hinders an affair that one was about to undertake, that might bring some dislike into one's heart, and he therefore asks Allāh to give him contentment.

SEEKING ADVICE

We seen from the above *ḥadīth* that, in addition to *istikhārah*, it is recommended to consult with some knowledgeable people before making an important decision.

Thus it is recommended for the man and woman (or her *walī*) to investigate about his or her intended partner, making sure that she or he has the required good attributes.

When a person's advice is sought in regard to individuals that are considered for marriage, business partnership, etc, he should provide truthful and honest advice. This advice should be limited to matters relevant to the affair in question, and should not be exceeded to other areas because that may then count as a prohibited form of backbiting.

Fāṭimah Bint Qays (ﷺ) reported that her husband ʿAmr Bin Ḥafṣ (ﷺ) went to a fight in al-Yaman (Yemen) with ʿAlī Bin Abī Ṭālib (ﷺ). While he was away, he sent ʿAyyāsh Bin Abī Rabīʿah to deliver to her a third and final divorce, and he sent with him a quantity of dates and barley as a present. She protested to ʿAyyāsh and requested more support but he responded, "By Allāh, you do not deserve a support unless you were pregnant." She went complaining to Allāh's Messenger (ﷺ), and he asked her, «كم طلّقكِ؟» **‹How many**

1 Recorded by al-Bukhārī and others.

times did he divorce you?› She replied, "Three times." He said, «صدق، ليس لكِ عليه نفقة.» **‹He is right then — he does not owe you any support (because the marriage was terminal).›**

The Prophet (ﷺ) told her to spend her *'iddah* in Umm Sharīk's house, but then remembered that some of his male companions go into her house. So he said:

«اَعتدّي في بيت ابن عمِّك عبدِ اللّهِ ابنِ أمِّ مكتوم، فإنه رجلٌ ضريرُ البصر، وإنكِ إذا وضعتِ ثيابَكِ (أو خمارَكِ) لم يركِ. فإذا انقضت عِدَّتُكِ فآذِنيني.»

> **‹Spend your *'iddah* in the house of your cousin 'Abdullāh Ibn Umm Maktūm's. Indeed, he is a blind man, and when you remove your head-cover, he would not see you. When you complete your *'iddah*, inform me.›**

When she completed her *'iddah*, Fāṭimah went to the Prophet (ﷺ) and told him that both Mu'āwiyah Bin Abī Sufyān and Abū Jahm asked for her hand. Allāh's Messenger (ﷺ) said:

«أما أبو جهم، فمنه شدةٌ على النساء ولا يضع العصا عن عاتقه، وأما مُعاوية فصعلوكٌ (أو تَربٌ) خفيفُ الحال (أو لا مال عنده.)، انكَحي أسامةَ بنَ زيد.»

> **‹As for Abū Jahm, he is harsh with women, and never takes the stick off his shoulder; and as for Mu'āwiyah, he is a poor man without any money. Marry Usāmah Bin Zayd.›**

She disliked that, but the Prophet (ﷺ) repeated, «انكَحي أسامةَ بنَ زيد.» **‹Marry Usāmah Bin Zayd.›** She concluded:

> "Then I married Usāmah; Allāh put a great deal of good

in him, and I was very happy with him." [1]

Telling the Truth

As we indicated above, it is important to provide truthful information in regard to the two individuals involved in a *khiṭbah*. The information should be limited to matters that are expected to have a bearing on the marriage. Absolute truth is required from the two involved parties: the man seeking to marry and the woman being sought, as well as their representatives, and any other individuals who are asked for advice.

Hiding any problems that one knows about is a sinful act of mistrust in *Islām*, and could result in numerous future predicaments.

For instance, one is required to indicate any physical problem in the two individuals involved in the *khiṭbah*. If either of them has a physical deficiency, such as impotence, venereal diseases, etc, he (or she) should make it known to the other individual before approving the engagements.

As for the one who thus learns about some problems in the other person, he is not allowed to publicize that knowledge or expose those secrets.

Violations in *Khiṭbah*

There are many violations that some Muslims have introduced into the process of *khiṭbah*. Many of those violations arise from blind imitation of the non-Muslims. In what follows we mention a few of them:

1. After the engagement, and before the marriage contract, the woman's family permit her to go out with the "fiancée", have *khulwah* with him, and even touch and kiss him.

2. Some people think of the engagement as a "test-drive" period in which they fully try out their partners to see if they will be able to pursue a long life together. With that, they commit many sins,

1 Recorded by Muslim, Abū Dāwūd, and others.

minor and major, including *zinā*. And interestingly, many of those engagements prove unsuccessful and end up in separation before marriage!

3. Some families like to extend the engagement period to months or even years, thereby providing more chance for the engaged couple to fall into sinning.

4. In many Muslim countries, the *khiṭbah* is held publicly in the form of a reception or party in which drinks are served, music is played, and the bridegroom kisses the bride or takes pictures with her. All of that is in great discord with the *Sunnah* and the *Islām*ic teachings, and should therefore be totally avoided. A *khiṭbah* should stay away from the people's eyes because no legal *sharʿī* consequences result from it. If, for any reason, a publicized *khiṭbah* is not concluded with actual marriage, serious harm may result from publicizing it, especially in regard to the bride's reputation.

5. The engaged couple often exchange "engagement" rings, and the bridegroom gives the bride jewelry and gifts at the time of *khiṭbah*. This too is in violation of *Islām*, since there is no reason yet for any property or gift exchange to take place — until they are legally bound by the marriage contract. In many cases, this premature act leads to serious disputes if the engagement is broken for any reason. Furthermore, the "engagement" ring has no basis in *Islām*. It originates from an old Christian practice that the Muslims should not imitate.

CHAPTER 4

THE MARRIAGE CONTRACT

Introduction

Importance of the Marriage Contract

The marriage (or *nikāḥ*) contract is enacted between a man and woman for the purpose of enjoying each other and forming a good family.

The marriage contract is the formal bond that turns two individuals from strangers to husband and wife. As a result of the marriage contract, many rights and obligations become imperative and many fruits become anticipated.

The marriage contract is the most important contract that most people execute throughout their lives. Each marriage contract normally carries a lasting effect over a large number of individuals many of them are yet to be born.

Since the marriage contract has such a great and solemn significance, *Islām* imposes a number of guidelines that it must fulfill. Those guidelines are the subject of discussion in this chapter.

No Joking in Marriage

Marriage is a serious matter and should be dealt with seriously. It is not allowed for a man to marry and then claim that he did not really mean it or that he was joking.

Abū Hurayrah (ﷺ) reported that Allāh's Messenger (ﷺ) said:

«ثلاثٌ جِدُّهنَّ جِد وهَزلُهنَّ جِد: النكاحُ، والطلاق، والرجعة.»

‹There are three matters that are considered serious in both serious and joking talks: marriage, divorce, and returning (a wife who was divorced a non-

terminal divorce).› [1]

Fuḍālah Bin ʿUbayd (ﷺ) reported that Allāh's Messenger (ﷺ) said:

«ثلاثٌ لا يجوز اللعبُ فيهن: الطلاقُ والنكاح والعتق.»

‹There are three matters in which it is not permissible to joke: marriage, divorce, and emancipation (of slaves).› [2]

Basic Elements

The *Islām*ic marriage contract has conditions, requirements, pillars, and optional elements. A contract must fulfill the conditions and pillars in order to be valid. The following are the elements commonly specified by the scholars:

a) Conditions:
- The bridegroom's eligibility for that marriage
- The bride's eligibility for that marriage
- The bridegroom's consent
- The bride's permission
- The *walī*'s presence or approval
- The presence of at least two male Muslim trustworthy witnesses

b) Requirements
- The dowry

c) Pillars
- The offering (*ījāb*)
- The acceptance (*qabūl*)

1 Recorded by Abū Dāwūd, at-Tirmiḏhī, and others. Verified to be *ḥasan* by al-Albānī (*Irwāʾ ul-Ghalīl* no. 1826 & *Ṣaḥīḥ ul-Jāmiʿ* no. 3027).

2 Recorded by aṭ-Ṭabarānī (in *al-Kabīr*). Verified to be *ḥasan* by al-Albānī (*Irwāʾ ul-Ghalīl* no. 1826 & *Ṣaḥīḥ ul-Jāmiʿ* no. 3047).

d) Optional Elements
- The conditions

These elements are discussed in the following sections.

The Bridegroom

The bridegroom is the man who seeks to marry. To be eligible for marriage, the bridegroom must fulfill the following requirements:

a) He must be Muslim.
b) He should be chaste.
c) He should be a male who has attained puberty.
d) He should have full mental ability.
e) He must not be related to the bride by any of the permanently prohibiting blood, milk, or marital relationships (as discussed in Chapter 8).
f) He must not be prohibited from marrying the bride for any of the temporary reasons (as discussed in Chapter 8).

Furthermore, the bridegroom must be performing the marriage contact willingly and may not be forced.

The Bride

The bride should fulfill the following requirements:

a) She should be chaste.
b) She must be Muslim, Christian or Jew.
c) She should have full mental ability.
d) She must not be married to another man.
e) She must not be related to the groom by any of the permanently prohibiting blood, milk, or marital relationships (as discussed in Chapter 8).
f) She must not be prohibited from marrying the groom for any of the temporary reasons (as discussed in Chapter 8).

The Bride's Permission

RULING

Being one of the two individuals involved in a marriage contract, the bride should have a say in regard to the partner with whom she would be associated in a long-term partnership.

'Ā'ishah (🖾) reported that Allāh's Messenger (🖼) said:

«استأمروا النساء في أبضاعهن. »

‹Take the women's permission in regard to their private parts (i.e., marriage).› [1]

Abū Mūsā al-Ash'arī (🖾) reported that Allāh's Messenger (🖼) said:

«إذا أراد أحدكم يزوج ابنته فليستأمرها. »

‹When one of you wants to give his daughter in marriage, he should take her permission.› [2]

A bride's permission is a required element of the marriage contract. Without this permission, the contract is either null and void, or may be invalidated by the *Islāmic* authorities — based on the bride's request.

We will see below that, depending on the bride's situation, the mode of her permission varies from being fully vocal and assertive to being passive and compliant with her *walī*'s decision.

A VIRGIN BRIDE

A virgin bride (in Arabic: *bikr*) is a woman who never had intercourse

---

1 Recorded by Aḥmad and an-Nasā'ī. Verified to be authentic by al-Albānī (*Ṣaḥīḥ ul-Jāmi'* no. 930 & *aṣ-Ṣaḥīḥah* no. 398).

2 Recorded by aṭ-Ṭabarānī (in *al-Kabīr*) and Abū Ya'lā. Verified to be authentic by al-Albānī (*Ṣaḥīḥ ul-Jāmi'* no. 300 & *aṣ-Ṣaḥīḥah* no. 1206).

with men. That would normally mean that her virginity hymen is present and intact; however, this is not an absolute condition because some virgins may lose their hymen in an accident or illness.

A virgin is usually naive and inexperienced in the ways of life and people's cunning. She has no knowledge about men and is unable to evaluate a potential husband. Thus, it is not possible for her to make a clear decision in that regard, and it is left for her *walī*, who is usually her father, to make the decision on her behalf. Even then, he must consult with her and take her approval before executing the marriage contract.

When a virgin is adorned with the strong *ḥayā'* (modesty and shyness) that adorned the early Muslim virgins, she would be extremely reluctant to voice her opinion in regard to a man who seeks to marry her. In that case, her passive expression of approval is sufficient.

A passive approval is expressed by the bride's remaining silent, nodding her head, or making any other motion to indicate that she does not object to the marriage. On the other hand, if she does object, she must declare that with a clear action or statement.

The bride's passive approval is the minimum required permission. However, it is possible for her to express her approval in a more assertive way, such as saying, "Yes, I would like to marry him."

Abū Hurayrah (ﷺ) reported that the Prophet (ﷺ) said:

«لا تُنكَحُ الثيّبُ (الأيّمُ) حتى تُستأمر، ولا تُنكحُ البكر حتى تُستأذنَ، وإذنها الصموت (أن تسكت).»

‹A deflowered unmarried woman (i.e. widow or divorcee) may not be married without her instructions; and a virgin may not be married without her permission, and her silence indicates her consent.› [1]

'Umayrah al-Kindī (ﷺ) reported that Allāh's Messenger (ﷺ) said:

1 Recorded by al-Bukhārī, Muslim, and others.

«آمروا النساء في أنفسهنَّ، فأنَّ الثيّبَ تُعربُ عن نفسِها (بلِسانِها)، والبِكرُ رضاها صمتها (صِماتُها)».

‹Take the women's permission in regard to themselves (i.e., marriage). A non-virgin expresses herself with her tongue; and a virgin's silence is (a sufficient proof of) her acceptance.› [1]

Ibn ʿAbbās (ﷺ) reported:

"A virgin woman came to the Prophet (ﷺ) and told him that her father gave her in marriage against her will. The Prophet (ﷺ) then gave her the choice (of maintaining or terminating the marriage)." [2]

A Deflowered Bride

A non-virgin or deflowered bride (in Arabic: *thayyib*) is a woman who has had at least one sexual intercourse with men — whether it was in regular marriage or *zinā*.

A *thayyib* normally has more experience in life and more ability to make a decision in regard to her marriage. Thus, she should be allowed to voice her opinion and make her decision, and her decision must be honored by her *walī*. This is clearly expressed in the above *ḥadīth*s. Similarly, Ibn ʿAbbāṣ (ﷺ) reported that Allāh's Messenger (ﷺ) said:

«الثيِّبُ (الأيِّم) أحقُّ بنفسها من وليِّها، والبكر تُستأذن في نفسها، وإذنُها صُماتها».

‹A non-virgin has more right to herself than does her guardian; as for a virgin, her permission is taken in regard to herself, and her silence is (a sufficient)

1 Recorded by Aḥmad, Ibn Mājah, and others. Verified to be authentic by al-Albānī (*Ṣaḥīḥ ul-Jāmiʿ* no. 13, 3084 & *Irwāʾ ul-Ghalīl* no. 1836).

2 Recorded by Ibn Mājah. Verified to be authentic by al-Albānī (*Ṣaḥīḥ Ibn Mājah* no. 1520).

permission.> [1]

Al-Khansā' Bint Khithām al-Anṣariyyah (☺) reported that her father gave her in marriage (without her permission). At that time, she was non-virgin. She disliked that marriage and complained to the Prophet (☺) who invalidated the contract. [2]

AN ORPHAN BRIDE

An orphan girl is a virgin who lost her father. Thus, her *walī* is not her father. In regard to the permission for marriage, she is given more say than a normal virgin.

Abū Mūsā al-Ash'arī (☺) reported that Allāh's Messenger (☺) said:

«آمروا اليتيمة في نفسها، وإذنها صماتها.»

‹Give a (virgin) orphan girl the right to decide in regard to herself (in marriage), and her silence is (a sufficient) permission.› [3]

Abū Hurayrah (☺) reported that Allāh's Messenger (☺) said:

«تُستأمر اليتيمةُ في نفسها، فإن سكتت (صمتت)

فهو إذنُها، وإن أبت فلا جوازَ عليها.»

‹A (virgin) orphan girl's permission should be sought in regard to herself (i.e., in marriage); if she remains silent, that counts as her permission; and if she expresses her refusal, she may not be forced against her will.› [4]

---

1 Recorded by Muslim, Abū Dāwūd, and others.

2 Recorded by al-Bukhārī, Aḥmad, and others.

3 Recorded by aṭ-Ṭabarānī, Aḥmad, and others. Verified to be authentic by al-Albānī (*Ṣaḥīḥ ul-Jāmi'* no. 14 & *aṣ-Ṣaḥīḥah* no. 656).

4 Recorded by Abū Dāwūd, an-Nasā'ī, and others. Verified to be authentic by al-Albānī (*Ṣaḥīḥ ul-Jāmi'* no. 1349, 8194 & *Irwā' ul-Ghalīl* no. 1834).

'Abdullāh Bin 'Umar (   ) reported that when 'Uthmān Bin Maẓ'ūn (   ) died he left behind a daughter from his wife Khuwaylah Bint Ḥakīm. In his will, 'Uthmān had appointed his brother Qudāmah Bin Maẓ'ūn as her guardian. Ibn 'Umar asked for the orphan girl's hand from Qudāmah (who was his maternal uncle), and Qudāmah agreed to marry her to him. However, al-Mughīrah Bin Shu'bah (   ) approached her mother and beguiled her with money. The mother thus leaned toward him, and her daughter followed her mother's inclination and refused to marry 'Abdullāh. They disputed and went before the Prophet (   ). Qudāmah said:

> "O Allāh's Messenger! She is my brother's daughter. He appointed me as her guardian, and I gave her in marriage to 'Abdullāh Bin 'Umar. Thus, I forsook in that neither righteousness nor compatibility. However, she is only a woman, and she now leans according to her mother's inclination."

Allāh's Messenger (   ) responded:

$$ \text{«هِيَ يَتِيمَةٌ، وَلَا تُنكَحُ إِلَّا بِإِذْنِهَا.»} $$

‹She is an orphan, and she may not be married except with her permission.›

Ibn 'Umar added:

> "Thus, by Allāh, she was taken away from me, even after I had taken charge of her (by marriage), and was married to al-Mughīrah Bin Shu'bah." [1]

A FREED SLAVE WOMAN

If a married couple were both slaves, and the woman is freed first, she would be given the option of staying with her husband or leaving him.

---

1   Recorded by Aḥmad, ad-Dāraquṭnī, and others. Verified to be *ḥasan* by al-Albānī (*Irwā'ul-Ghalīl* no. 1835).

If she makes the first choice, she remains married to him and would have no further chance in that regard.

Barīrah was a slave woman owned by some of *al-Anṣār*. She was married to a black slave called Mughīth.

ʿĀ'ishah (ﷺ) reported that Allāh's Messenger (ﷺ) told her in regard to Barīrah, «خذيها فأعتقيها.» **‹Take her and free her.›** So she bought her from her owners and freed her. Allāh's Messenger (ﷺ) then gave her the choice of remaining married to her husband or going on her own. She chose to be on her own. [1]

ʿĀ'ishah (ﷺ) also reported that when Allāh's Messenger (ﷺ) gave Barīrah the choice he told her, «إن قربكِ فلا خِيارَ لكِ.» **‹If he approaches you, then you will have no choice.›** [2]

Barīrah's departure broke Mugīth's heart. Ibn ʿAbbās (ﷺ) narrated, "It is as if I still see him following her in the streets of al-Madīnah, crying until his tears wet his beard." Allāh's Messenger (ﷺ) said:

«يا عباس! ألا تعجبُ من حب مغيثٍ بَريرةَ،

ومن بغض بريرةَ مُغيثاً؟»

> **‹O ʿAbbās! Does it not surprise you how much Mughīth loves Barīrah, and how much Barīrah dislikes Mughīth?›**

The Prophet (ﷺ) then said to Barīrah, «لو راجعته.» **‹Would you consider taking him back?›** She said, "O Allāh's Messenger, is this a command?" He said, «إنما أشفعُ.» **‹I am only interceding (for his sake).›** She said, "I have no interest in him then." [3]

---

1 Recorded by al-Bukhārī, Muslim, and others.

2 Recorded by Abū Dāwūd. Verified to be authentic by al-Albānī (*al-Mishkāt* no. 3201).

3 Recorded by al-Bukhārī and others.

The Woman's *Walī*

RULING

A woman may not independently give herself in marriage. Her *walī* (guardian) should represent her in doing that. He should take her consent if she is a virgin. Otherwise, he should follow her instruction.

Abū Mūsā al-Ashʿarī, ʿAbdullāh Bin ʿAbbās, Jābir Bin ʿAbdillāh, and Abū Hurayrah (﴾) reported that Allāh's Messenger (﴿) said:

$$ «لا نكاح إلا بولي.» $$

‹A marriage (contract) is not valid without a *walī*.› [1]

Thus, the presence of the *walī* for the execution of the marriage contract is a condition for its validity.

WHO IS A WOMAN'S *WALĪ*?

Normally, a woman's *walī* is her father. If, for any reason, her father is unable to be her *walī*, her *walī* would then be her next closest *maḥram* (grandfather, son, brother, uncle, etc).

If the woman's close relatives are non-Muslims, they may not be her *sharʿī* guardians. Allāh (﴿) says:

$$ ﴿وَلَن يَجْعَلَ ٱللَّهُ لِلْكَـٰفِرِينَ عَلَى ٱلْمُؤْمِنِينَ سَبِيلًا ۞﴾ النساء ١٤١ $$

«Allāh will never grant to the unbelievers a way (of authority) over the believers» [2]

A woman may not take another woman as her *walī*. Abū Hurayrah (﴾) reported that Allāh's Messenger (﴿) said:

$$ «لا تُزَوِّجُ المرأةُ المرأةَ، ولا تُزوجُ المرأةُ نفسَها.» $$

---

1   Recorded by Abū Dāwūd, at-Tirmithī, and others. Verified to be authentic by al-Albānī (*Irwāʾul-Ghalīl* no. 1839).

2   *An-Nisāʾ* 4:141.

"فإن الزانيةَ هي التي تُزَوِّج نفسَها."

‹A woman may not give another woman in marriage, nor may a woman give herself (independently) in marriage.›

Abū Hurayrah (ﷺ) added:

"For, indeed, it is an adulteress who gives herself in marriage (without her *walī*'s consent)." [1]

If the bride does not have a Muslim blood-relative as *walī*, the *Islām*ic authority, represented by the ruler or judge, would appoint a *walī* for her. In many non-Muslim countries, the local *imām* of a Muslim community carries out the common duties of an *Islām*ic judge, and would therefore be the *walī* of a woman who has no *walī*.

'Ā'ishah (ﷺ) reported that Allāh's Messenger (ﷺ) said:

«لا نكاح إلا بولي، والسلطان وليٌّ من لا وليَّ له.»

‹A marriage (contract) is not valid without a *walī*. And the (*Islām*ic) authority is the *walī* of the one who does not have a *walī*.› [2]

A Woman May Not Appoint Her *Walī*

A common practice in many non-*Islām*ic countries is that a woman, having no Muslim *maḥram* as *walī*, would appoint her own *walī*. This is wrong, and she has no right to do so. As we have seen above, this is the right of the *Islām*ic judge or *imām*.

This incorrect practice has caused a number of bad consequences, among which are the following:

---

1 Recorded by Ibn Mājah, al-Bayhaqī, and others. Verified to be authentic by al-Albānī (*Irwā'ul-Ghalīl* no. 1841).

2 Recorded by Aḥmad, Abū Dāwūd, and others. Verified to be authentic by al-Albānī (*Irwā'ul-Ghalīl* no. 1840).

1. The appointed *walī* is often found unworthy of the trust invested in him and incapable of properly serving his principal's interests.

2. Some women take liberty in dealing with the *walī*. They treat him as an intimate friend or relative, often sharing with him intimate secrets and going into *khulwah* (complete privacy) with him, which often leads to committing major sins.

3. Some women expect from the *walī* much more than what is within his capacity. His only duty is representing the woman and serving her best interest in regard to the marriage negotiations and contract. Once that is done, his duty ends and he stops being her *walī*. Some women, though, think that the *walī*'s position is permanent, and they contact him for every little or big problem in their life. This results in a relationship that is quite intimate and may lead to serious sinning as in (2) above.

MARRIAGE WITHOUT A *WALĪ*

From the above, we conclude that the presence of the *walī* (or his representative) is a required condition for the validity of the marriage contract. Therefore, a marriage that is held without the *walī*'s consent and approval is null and void.

'Āishah (رضي الله عنها) reported that the Messenger (ﷺ) said:

«أيما امرأةٍ نكحت بغير إذن وليها، فنكاحها باطل، فنكاحها باطل، فنكاحها باطل. فإن دخل بها فلها المهر بما استحل من فرجها. فإن اشتجروا، فالسلطان وليُّ من لا وليَّ له.»

‹Whichever woman marries without her *walī*'s permission, her marriage is void, her marriage is void, her marriage is void. If he (the husband) performs intercourse with her (despite the invalidity of their marriage), the *mahr* becomes her right because he had access to her private parts. And if they dispute (with the *walī* about this or other

matters), the ruler would then be the *walī* of the one
who does not have a *walī*.» [1]

A HARD-TO-DEAL-WITH *WALĪ*

A *walī* is required to represent his principal and serve her best interest.
From the above *ḥadīth* of 'Ā'ishah (◌), we see that if the *walī* causes
unnecessary harm to his principal or prevents her from doing things
that Allāh has made permissible for her, she may protest and dispute
that before the *Islāmic* authorities. In that case, and if her allegations
were found true, the *Islāmic* judge may command the *walī* to change
his course of action, may remove the guardianship from him and
transfer it to some other man, or may make some other decisions as he
sees fit in her case.

Ma'qil Bin Yasār (◌) reported that he married his sister to a man
who subsequently divorced her. After the end of her *'iddah*, he came
seeking to remarry her. Ma'qil said to him, "I married her to you, gave
you furnishings, and was generous to you, but you divorced her! No,
by Allāh, she will never go back to you!" But the man was reasonably
good, and the woman wanted to go back to him. Allāh (◌) then
revealed:

$$﴿وَإِذَا طَلَّقْتُمُ ٱلنِّسَاءَ فَبَلَغْنَ أَجَلَهُنَّ فَلَا تَعْضُلُوهُنَّ أَن يَنكِحْنَ$$
$$أَزْوَاجَهُنَّ إِذَا تَرَاضَوْاْ بَيْنَهُم بِٱلْمَعْرُوفِ﴾ البقرة ٢٣٢$$

**«And when you divorce women and they have
fulfilled their term, do not prevent them from
remarrying their husbands — if they agree between
themselves on reasonable terms.»** [2]

Ma'qil then said to Allāh's Messenger (◌), "Now I listen and obey,
O Allāh's Messenger!" So he let them remarry, and expiated his oath. [3]

---

1   Recorded by Aḥmad, Abū Dāwūd, and others. Verified to be authentic by al-
     Albānī (*Irwā'ul-Ghalīl* no. 1840).

2   *Al-Baqarah* 2:232.

3   Recorded by al-Bukhārī, ad-Dāraquṭnī, and others.

THE *WALĪ'S* RESPONSIBILITY

The *walī*, whether natural or appointed, holds a major responsibility before Allāh toward his principal. He should represent her and look after her interest in the best possible way. He should make sure that the man who seeks marrying her is suitable for her. His criteria should be what pleases Allāh (as has been outlined in Chapter 2), and not what brings him better social status, wealth, or other worldly gains.

If it is demonstrated that the *walī* is not worthy of his responsibility, he loses his *walāyah* (position as being *walī*) according to the procedure outlined earlier.

The Witnesses

Another condition for the validity of a marriage contract is the presence of at least two trustworthy Muslim male witnesses.

ʿĀ'ishah, ʿImrān Bin Ḥaṣayn, and Abū Mūsā al-Ashʿarī (ﷺ) reported that the Prophet (ﷺ) said:

«لا نكاح إلا بولي وشاهدي عدل.»

‹A marriage (contract) is not valid without a *walī* and two trustworthy witnesses.› [1]

The witnesses should witness and hear all of the contract's details, including the permission given by the bride to the *walī*.

The *Mahr* (Dowry)

DEFINITION AND RULING

In *Islām*, the dowry is a mandatory marriage gift given by the husband to his wife at wedding. In Arabic, it is called *mahr* or *ṣadāq*.

---

1 Recorded by Aḥmad, Ibn Ḥibbān, and others. Verified to be authentic by al-Albānī (*Irwā'ul-Ghalīl* no. 1839, 1858, 1860).

Allāh (ﷻ) commands:

﴿وَءَاتُواْ ٱلنِّسَآءَ صَدُقَـٰتِهِنَّ نِحْلَةً﴾ النساء ٤

«And give the women (upon marriage) their dowry as a free gift.» [1]

Commenting on this *āyah*, al-Qurṭubī (رحمه الله) said:

> "This *āyah* indicates that the woman's *ṣadāq* is mandatory. There is a consensus on this (among the scholars), and there is no difference in its regard …" [2]

And Allāh (ﷻ) commands:

﴿فَـَٔاتُوهُنَّ أُجُورَهُنَّ فَرِيضَةً﴾ النساء ٢٤

«And give them (the women that you marry) their compensation as an obligation.» [3]

And Allāh (ﷻ) commands:

﴿فَٱنكِحُوهُنَّ بِإِذْنِ أَهْلِهِنَّ، وَءَاتُوهُنَّ أُجُورَهُنَّ بِٱلْمَعْرُوفِ﴾ النساء ٢٥

«So marry them (slave girls) with their people's permission, and give them their compensation according to what is reasonable.» [4]

Even though the *mahr* is an obligation on the husband, there is no proof to make it a condition for the validity of the marriage contract. As we will see below, a marriage contract could possibly be executed without specifying a *mahr*. However, that should normally be avoided because it may lead to future complications and disputes.

---

1 *An-Nisā'* 4:4.

2 *Al-Jāmi'u li-Aḥkām il-Qur'ān.*

3 *An-Nisā'* 4:24.

4 *An-Nisā'* 4:25.

WHO TAKES THE *MAHR*

The *mahr* is the sole right of the wife and no one may take any of it without her permission — not even her parents.

Some people may object to the above by citing the story of the old man who offered his daughter to Mūsā (ﷺ) and took her dowry in the form of labor work from Mūsā (see p. 50). However, aṣ-San'ānī indicates that that was possibly permissible in the laws prior to *Islām* but was abrogated in *Islām* [1]. Furthermore, Mūsā's service to the old man may have profited Mūsā's wife as well. Also, she may have agreed with her father to take something from him in exchange for Mūsā's service.

The *mahr* is a compensation that the wife takes in return for making herself available to her husband. Thus, Allāh (ﷻ) gives her full right to it, even at the time of divorce — if her husband divorces her without any default on her part. Allāh (ﷻ) says:

﴿وَإِنْ أَرَدتُّمُ ٱسْتِبْدَالَ زَوْجٍ مَّكَانَ زَوْجٍ وَءَاتَيْتُمْ إِحْدَاهُنَّ قِنطَارًا فَلَا تَأْخُذُوا۟ مِنْهُ شَيْـًٔا ۚ أَتَأْخُذُونَهُۥ بُهْتَـٰنًا وَإِثْمًا مُّبِينًا ۝ وَكَيْفَ تَأْخُذُونَهُۥ وَقَدْ أَفْضَىٰ بَعْضُكُمْ إِلَىٰ بَعْضٍ وَأَخَذْنَ مِنكُم مِّيثَـٰقًا غَلِيظًا ۝﴾ النساء ٢٠-٢١

«If you want to substitute one wife for another, and you have given one of them a *qinṭār* [2], do not take back any of it. Would you take it in injustice and manifest sin? And how could you take it while you have intimately dealt with each other, and they (your wives) have taken from you a solemn covenant?» [3]

We will show below that the "*qinṭār*" in this *āyah* does not only

1 *Subul us-Salām*.

2 *Qinṭār*: According to *Lisān ul-'Arab*, it is a large indefinite quantity of gold or silver. Most commonly, the Arabs used to mean by it four-thousand *dīnārs* (or gold coins).

3 *An-Nisā'* 4:20.

refer to the *mahr*, but also to all gifts and other things that the husband gives to the wife whom he then wants to divorce without a reason.

Therefore, it is up to the wife if she wants to keep all of her *mahr*, give some of it to her parents or other people, or even give some of it back to her husband [1]. Allāh (ﷻ) says:

﴿وَءَاتُوا۟ ٱلنِّسَآءَ صَدُقَـٰتِهِنَّ نِحْلَةً ۚ فَإِن طِبْنَ لَكُمْ عَن شَىْءٍ مِّنْهُ نَفْسًا فَكُلُوهُ هَنِيٓـًٔا مَّرِيٓـًٔا ۝﴾ النساء ٤

«And give the women (upon marriage) their dowry as a free gift. But if they give up willingly to you any of it, then enjoy it with pleasure and satisfaction.» [2]

KINDS

The dowry can be money, jewelry, clothes, or other material things. It can also be a non-material gift, as we'll see below.

The amount of the dowry should be in accordance with the husband's financial ability and with what is reasonable for the bride in her social status. It is normally determined by agreement between the husband and the bride (or her *walī*).

Sahl Bin Saʿd (ﷺ) reported that a woman once came to the Prophet (ﷺ) and offered herself (in marriage) to him. He (ﷺ) declined and indicated that he had no need for any (additional) wives. A man who was present with him said, "O Allāh's Messenger! Marry her to me." The Prophet (ﷺ) asked him, «هل عندك من شيء؟» **‹Do you have anything (to give her)?›** He said, "No!" The Prophet (ﷺ) said, «أعطها ولو خاتما من حديد.» **‹Give her at least an iron ring.›** But he still could not afford it. He (ﷺ) asked him, «هل معك من القرآن شيء؟» **‹Do you memorize any portion of the *Qurʾān*?›** He replied, "I memorize such-and-such *sūrahs*." The Prophet (ﷺ) then said:

---

1 Note that the way a woman dispenses of any of her property would still be subject to her husband's approval. For more information in this regard, one is directed to the third part of this series, "The Fragile Vessels", by the author.

2 *An-Nisāʾ* 4:4.

«أذهب فقد أنكحتُكها بما معك من القرآن.»

‹Go (have her as wife). I marry her to you for the portion of the *Qur'ān* that you memorize.› [1]

One may ask, "What benefit did she get from his memorization of the *Qur'ān*?" The answer is that he would then be expected to teach her some of what he had memorized, and to treat her kindly based on what he had memorized. All of that would be of much more benefit to the bride than lots of material gifts.

In addition to a cash sum of money that is usually specified as the *mahr*, some cultures require from the husband other financial commitments toward the bride, such as clothes, jewelry, and so on. In the *Islām*ic *law, a*ll of that counts as part of the *mahr*, and it is best to clearly name it in the marriage contract to avoid future disputes.

Moderateness in Dowries

Islām does not set an upper limit for the dowry; but it is recommended to make it light and easy on the husband. A burdening *mahr* could be a bad omen of a miserable and non-compassionate marriage.

In many Muslim countries, the woman's parents request extremely high dowries. That has led many young men to forsake marriage or postpone it for a number of years, which has in turn led to the spread of *zinā* and other sins among the young. Thus, the parents should be considerate and should realize that demanding too much from the husband brings harm to their daughters and the whole Muslim community.

Abū Hurayrah (ﷺ) reported that a man came to the Prophet (ﷺ) and said, "I have married a woman from *al-Anṣār*." [2] The Prophet (ﷺ) asked him, «على كم تزوجتها؟» **‹How much (*mahr*) you gave her?›** He replied, "Four *ūqiyyahs* [3]." Noting his limited financial condition, and that he needed help paying that *mahr*, the Prophet (ﷺ) said

---

1 Recorded by al-Bukhārī, Muslim, and others.

2 This is the same man that the Prophet (ﷺ) asked if he had looked at his bride before marrying her (see p. 40).

3 *Ūqiyyah*: An old measure that corresponded to forty *dirhams*.

disapprovingly:

«على أربع أواق؟ كأنما تنحتون الفضة من عُرض هذا الجبل.»

‹Four *ūqiyyahs*? It is as though you scoop silver from the side of this mountain!› [1]

Abū Ḥadrad al-Aslamī (ﷺ) reported that he came to the Prophet (ﷺ) seeking help in paying a woman's *mahr*. The Prophet (ﷺ) asked him, «كم أمهرتَها؟» **‹How much you promised to give her?›** He replied, "Two hundred *dirhams*." The Prophet (ﷺ) responded:

«لو كنتم تغرفون من بَطحانِ ما زدتم.»

‹Had you been scooping (silver) from Baṭḥān [2], you would not have pledged more than that.› [3]

'Uqbah Bin 'Āmir (ﷺ) reported that Allāh's Messenger (ﷺ) said:

«خير النكاح (أو الصَّداق) أيسرُه.»

‹The best of marriages (or dowries) are the easiest.› [4]

A dowry that is light upon the husband is a sign of blessing for the bride. 'Ā'ishah (ﷺ) reported that Allāh's Messenger (ﷺ) said:

«إن من يُمنِ المرأة تيسيرُ خِطْبتِها، وتيسير صداقها، وتيسير رحِمِها.»

‹Verily, a sign of blessing for a woman is that her engagement, *ṣadāq*, and womb (i.e. giving birth), are

---

1 Recorded by Muslim, an-Nasā'ī, and others.

2 Name of a valley in al-Madīnah.

3 Recorded by al-Ḥākim and Aḥmad. Verified to be authentic by al-Albānī (*aṣ-Ṣaḥīḥah* no. 2173).

4 Recorded by Abū Dāwūd, Ibn Mājah, and others. Verified to be authentic by al-Albānī (*Ṣaḥīḥ ul-Jāmi'* no. 3279, 3300, *aṣ-Ṣaḥīḥah* no. 1842, & *Irwā' ul-Ghalīl* no. 1924).

all made easy.› [1]

UNSPECIFIED *MAHRS*

If the marriage contract is executed without specifying a *mahr*, that does not forfeit the wife's right to it.

'Uqbah Bin 'Āmir (🙼) reported that the Prophet (🙼) said to a man, «أترضى أن أزوجَك فلانة؟» ‹**Do you agree that I marry so-and-so woman to you?**› He replied, "Yes." The Prophet (🙼) then said to the woman, «أترضين أن أزوجَك فلاناً؟» ‹**Do you agree that I marry you to so-and-so man?**› She replied, "Yes." So he married them to each other without naming a *mahr* for the bride or giving her anything. That man was of those who witnessed al-Ḥudaybiyah Covenant, and he got a share from the battle spoils of Khaybar. When he approached death, he said:

> "Indeed, Allāh's Messenger (🙼) gave me so-and-so in marriage but I did not then give her anything. Be my witnesses that I now give her as *mahr* my share from Khaybar."

So she took that share and sold it for one hundred-thousand. [2]

'Ulqumah (🙼) reported that some people came to 'Abdullāh Bin Mas'ūd (🙼) and asked him about a case where one of them married a woman without naming a *mahr* for her and he died before consummating the marriage. 'Abdullāh said, "Since I departed from Allāh's Messenger (🙼), I have not been asked a harder question. Go ask someone else." They kept trying to get an answer from him for one month, at the end of which they said, "Whom would we ask if we do not ask you, and you are one of the most esteemed of Muḥammad's (🙼) companions in this land, and we cannot find anyone else?" He said, "I will try to give you my best opinion in her regard. If it is right, that would be from Allāh alone Who has no partners. And if it is wrong, that would be from me and from Satan, and Allāh and

---

1 Recorded by Aḥmad, al-Ḥākim, and others. Verified to be *ḥasan* by al-Albānī (*Ṣaḥīḥ ul-Jāmiʿ* no. 2235 & *Irwāʾ ul-Ghalīl* no. 1928).

2 Recorded by Abū Dāwūd, Ibn Ḥibbān, and others. Verified to be authentic by al-Albānī (*Irwāʾ ul-Ghalīl* no. 1924).

His Messenger would be clear from it." Then he said:

"لها صداق نسائها، لا وكسَ ولا شطط، وعليها العدةُ، ولها الميراثُ."

> "She should be given a *mahr* similar to that of other women of her family (or social status), without increase or reduction, and she should accomplish the ʿ*iddah* (of four months and ten days), and she should be given her share of the inheritance."

Some individuals from the tribe of Ashjaʿ were then present, and one of them called Maʿqil Bin Sinān al-Ashjaʿī stood and said:

> "I testify that your judgement is similar to what Allāh's Messenger (ﷺ) judged in regard to a woman of ours called Barūʿ Bint Wāshiq."

Since embracing *Islām*, ʿAbdullāh Bin Masʿūd was never seen as pleased as he was when he heard that. [1]

From the above reports we conclude that if, at wedding, a woman was not assigned a *mahr*, or if her *mahr* was too small compared to her husband's situation and the *mahr*s that are usually given to other women of her status, that does not forfeit her right to a fair *mahr*. She may then dispute that with the *Islām*ic authorities.

Therefore, extreme care should be taken by the woman's *walī* to make sure that his principal is given a fair *mahr* at the time of marriage. If she then chooses to give up part or all of it to the husband, she should do that voluntarily and knowingly.

Dowries of the Mothers of the Believers

The *mahr* that the Prophet (ﷺ) gave to his wives varied from one to another. In the case of Ṣafiyyah (رضي الله عنها), her dowry was emancipation from slavery. Anas (رضي الله عنه) reported:

---

1 Recorded by Abū Dāwūd, an-Nasāʾī, and others. Verified to be authentic by al-Albānī (*Irwāʾ ul-Ghalīl* no. 1939).

"أعتق النبي صفية، وجعل عِتقَها صَداقَها."

"The Prophet (ﷺ) freed Ṣafiyyah (and married her); and for dowry, he granted her freedom." [1]

Umm Ḥabībah (ﷺ) reported that she was married to ʿUbayd Ullāh Bin Jaḥsh, and he died when they were at al-Ḥabashah (Abyssinia). So an-Najāshī (the Abyssinian king) gave her to Allāh's Messenger (ﷺ) in marriage. On behalf of Allāh's Messenger (ﷺ), an-Najāshī gave her four thousand (*dirhams*) as *mahr*, and he then sent her to him with Sharḥabīl Bin Ḥasanah. [2]

Thus, Umm Ḥabībah's *mahr* was quite large. But it was not given to her by the Prophet (ﷺ) himself. Rather, it was a gift from an-Najāshī on his behalf. In all other cases, the *mahr* that Allāh's Messenger (ﷺ) gave to his wives did not exceed five hundred *dirhams*.

Abū Salamah ʿAbd ur-Raḥmān reported that he asked ʿĀʾishah (ﷺ), "How much was the *ṣadāq* of Allāh's Messenger (ﷺ)?" She replied:

"His *ṣadāq* to his wives was twelve and a half *ūqiyyahs*." [3]

Abū al-ʿAjfāʾ reported that ʿUmar (ﷺ) once gave a *khuṭbah* in which he said:

"لا تُغالوا في صدُقات النساء."

"Do not be excessive in regard to the women's dowries."

He (ﷺ) added:

"Had that been an indication of honor in this life or

1 Recorded by al-Bukhārī, Muslim, and others.

2 Recorded by Abū Dāwūd, an-Nasāʾī, and others. Verified to be authentic by al-Albānī (*Ṣaḥīḥ Abī Dāwūd* no. 1853).

3 Recorded by Muslim and others.

> *taqwā* before Allāh, the Prophet (ﷺ) would have been most worthy of it among you. Yet, Allāh's Messenger (ﷺ) did not give as dowry to any of his wives, nor did any of his daughters receive more than twelve *ūqiyyah*s." [1]

WEAK STORY: "A WOMAN IS RIGHT AND 'UMAR IS WRONG"

It is important to warn against a weak story that is alleged to having taken place between 'Umar and a woman. It is unfortunate to note that some great scholars, such as Ibn Taymiyyah (رحمه الله), have quoted this story without realizing its weakness.

Once 'Umar (رضي الله عنه) gave a speech in which he admonished against excessiveness in dowries and said, "I will not allow any dowry larger than that of the Prophet's (ﷺ) wives and daughters." A woman protested saying:

> "O Commander of the Believers! You just forbade the people from being excessive in dowries. Why would you prevent us from receiving something that Allāh (تعالى) gave us?"

She then recited:

﴿وَإِنْ أَرَدتُّمُ ٱسْتِبْدَالَ زَوْجٍ مَّكَانَ زَوْجٍ وَءَاتَيْتُمْ إِحْدَاهُنَّ قِنطَارًا
فَلَا تَأْخُذُوا۟ مِنْهُ شَيْـًٔا ۚ أَتَأْخُذُونَهُۥ بُهْتَـٰنًا وَإِثْمًا مُّبِينًا ۝﴾ النساء ٢٠

> **«If you want to substitute one wife for another, and you have given one of them a *qinṭār*, do not take back any of it. Would you take it in injustice and manifest sin?»** [2]

Upon hearing this, 'Umar said (two or three times), "All people

---

1 Recorded by Abū Dāwūd, an-Nasā'ī, and others. Verified to be authentic by al-Albānī (*Irwā' ul-Ghalīl* no. 1927).

2 *An-Nisā'* 4:20.

have a better understanding than ʿUmar. Indeed, a woman is right and ʿUmar is wrong!" Then he went back to the *minbar* (steps) and addressed the people saying:

> "Indeed, I have forbidden you from being excessive in the women's dowries. But now I say: let every man do with his wealth as he pleases." [1]

After indicating the weakness of this report, al-Albānī (ﷺ) said:

> "Furthermore, the woman's quotation of this *āyah* is out of place. The *āyah* refers to a woman who is divorced without reason. It means, 'If you wish to substitute a new wife for a previous one that you dislike and have no patience to treat with kindness — even though she did not commit any obvious sin, and if you had previously given her a large amount of money — whether she had received it all or you had pledged it to her, making it a debt owed by you to her, do not take back any of it. Rather, you should leave it all to its rightful owner. You only wish to substitute her with another woman for the sake of your desire and enjoyment, and not for any *sharʿī* reason that would have permitted your taking some of her money — such as her demanding separation, thereby hurting you by forcing you to divorce her. If she did not do anything like that, how can you take any of her money?'" [2]

This story is very commonly cited by speakers and writers, trying by doing so to prove a variety of points, some being absolutely false. Among the false conclusions are the following:

☛ There is nothing wrong with women standing in a *masjid* and

---

1 This is a combined report recorded by Abū Yaʿlā, al-Bayhaqī, and ʿAbd ur-Razzāq. It is declared to be extremely weak by al-Albānī (*Irwāʾ ul-Ghalīl* no. 1927 & *Raf ul-Malām* pp. 33-34).

2 Commentary on *Raf ul-Malām ʿan il-Aʾimmat il-Aʿlām* pp. 34-35.

correcting the *imām* or other speakers.

☞ Women may give public addresses to a mixed audience.

☞ No scholar of *Islām* deserves much respect, because even a common woman may easily expose his mistakes.

☞ Women should be allowed as members, or even heads, of religious councils, such as *shūrā* boards of *Islām*ic centers and organizations.

A POSSIBLE REASON FOR DESTRUCTION

Demanding from the husband *mahr* and gifts more than what he can afford could be a reason for destruction. If that becomes a standard practice among the people, it would inevitably lead some men to falling into theft, bribery, gambling, and other prohibited means in order to satisfy the greed of their wives and families. That would eventually destroy the whole society.

Abū Saʿīd al-Khudrī (⌘) reported that Allāh's Messenger (⌘) said:

«إن الدنيا حُلوةٌ خضرة، وإن اللَّهَ مستخلفُكم فيها فينظرُ كيف تعملون، فاتقوا الدنيا واتقوا النساءَ، فإن أول فتنةِ بني إسرائيل كانت في النساء.»

‹**Indeed, the *dunyā* (worldly life) is sweet and lush. And indeed, Allāh gives you custody over it to see how you will do. So, beware of the *dunyā*, and beware of women, because the first *fitnah* (trial) of the Children of Israel was through women.**› [1]

This *fitnah* is explained in another narration by Abū Saʿīd. He (⌘) said that once Allāh's Messenger (⌘) gave a long *khuṭbah* in which he spoke about incidents from this life and the Hereafter. Among those he mentioned was the following:

---

1   Recorded by Muslim and others.

«إن أول ما هلك بنو إسرائيل أن ٱمرأةَ الفقير كانت تُكلّفُهُ من الثياب

أو الصِّيَغِ ما تُكلّفُ ٱمرأةُ الغني ...»

‹Indeed, what first destroyed the Children of Israel is that a poor man's wife would require from him as much clothing and jewelry as a rich man's wife ...› [1]

POSTPONED *MAHR*

It is recommended to give the bride her *mahr* immediately after execution of the marriage contract. As we saw in the above examples, the Prophet (ﷺ) only asked the husband for what he could offer at the time of marriage, and not what he could pledge for a future date.

Yet, it is a very common practice to divide the *mahr* into two portions, an advanced portion paid at the execution of the marriage contract, and a postponed portion to be paid when divorce or death takes place between the spouses.

Postponing the *mahr* is, in general, an innovated inconvenience that departs from the normal practice in the *Sunnah.* It defeats the very purpose of *mahr*, which is to be a gift given to the bride prior to having any intimacy with her. It also burdens the husband with a large amount of money that he must pledge as a postponed debt to an indefinite term.

GREAT PUNISHMENT FOR TAKING AWAY A WOMAN'S *MAHR*

A woman's *mahr* is a serious debt in a man's neck. Thus, it is a major sin to take it away from her without her consent. Ibn ʿUmar (ﷺ) reported that Allāh's Messenger (ﷺ) said:

«أن أعظمَ الذنوب عند اللّهِ رجلٌ تزوج امرأةً، فلما قضى حاجتَه

منها طلّقها وذهب بمهرها. ورجلٌ استعمل رجلاً فذهب بأُجرتِه.

1 Recorded by Ibn Khuzaymah and Aḥmad. Verified to be authentic by al-Albānī (*aṣ-Ṣaḥīḥah* no. 591).

وآخرُ يقتل دابةً عبثاً . »

‹Indeed, among the greatest sins before Allāh is that of a man who marries a woman, and after he fulfills his need with her, he divorces her and takes her *mahr*; and a man who hires another man but does not give him his pay; and a man who kills an animal without reason.› [1]

This *ḥadīth* also points to a situation that is common in some of the Western countries. Some Muslims coming from other countries marry Western Muslim women for a slight *mahr*, and they enjoy them for some time and often obtain through them citizenship in their countries. Once they have fulfilled their needs from them, they divorce them with clear conscience!

This is totally wrong. They take advantage of their wives and, on top of that, underpay them their *mahr*s. They should fear Allāh and remember that if they get by this in this life, they will not be able to get by it before Allāh (ﷻ) on the Day of Judgement.

Conditions

Permissibility of Setting Conditions

At the time of enacting the marriage contract, the two parties may wish to set conditions whose violation would invalidate the contract. This is permissible and acceptable, as long as the conditions do not violate any *Islām*ic principles. The conditions are normally set by the wife's side, because the husband can terminate the marriage by uttering the divorce and needs no conditions to facilitate that for him.

ʿUqbah Bin ʿĀmir al-Juhanī (ﷺ) reported that the Prophet (ﷺ) said:

---

1 Recorded by al-Ḥākim and al-Bayhaqī. Verified to be *ḥasan* by al-Albānī (*Ṣaḥīḥ ul-Jāmiʿ* no. 1567 & *aṣ-Ṣaḥīḥah* no. 999).

«إن أحق الشروط أن تُوَفُّوا به ما استحللتم به الفروج.»

‹Verily, the conditions that deserve to be fulfilled the most are those which allow you access to the women's private parts (by marriage and intercourse).› [1]

POWER OF THE CONDITIONS

If the conditions are *Islām*ically acceptable, they must be fulfilled, and violating them would be sufficient cause for the wife to terminate the marriage if she so desires.

Al-Athram and ʿAbd ur-Raḥmān Bin Ghanam reported that a man married a woman and accepted her condition of wanting to stay in one house (i.e. town). Later on, he found it necessary to move to a different land, and his wife's family disputed that with ʿUmar (ﷺ). ʿUmar said, "Her condition must be honored." The man objected, "This is unfair to the men. So whenever a woman wishes to divorce her husband she would do so!" And ʿUmar replied:

"المؤمنون على شروطهم. مقاطع الحقوق عند الشروط."

"The believers are required to maintain their conditions; and the rights cease where there are conditions to fulfill." [2]

SUSPENDING A CONDITION

On the other hand, a condition may be waived by the wife, as an act of benevolence or forgiveness. Also, the *Islām*ic judge may suspend a condition if he finds that it could violate an *Islām*ic principle.

It is interesting to note that, in another cases, ʿUmar (ﷺ) suspended the same condition that he passed in the above narration. That could be due to some difference that he saw in the overall

---

1 Recorded by al-Bukhārī, Muslim, and others.

2 Recorded by Saʿīd Bin Mansūr, Ibn Abī Shaybah, al-Bayhaqī. Verified to be authentic by al-Albānī (*Irwāʾ ul-Ghalīl* no. 1893).

situation of the families between the two cases, leading him to different judgements (and Allāh (ﷻ) knows best).

Saʿīd Bin ʿUbayd Bin as-Sabbāq reported that a man who married during the time of ʿUmar allowed his wife a condition that he would not take her out (of her hometown). ʿUmar (رضي الله عنه) relieved him of this condition and said:

> "A woman should be with her husband (i.e., wherever he moves)." [1]

Commenting on this, al-Bayhaqī (رحمه الله) said:

> "This report is closer to the Book and *Sunnah*, and agrees with the opinion of others among the *ṣaḥābah* (رضي الله عنهم)."

VOID CONDITIONS

As indicated above, if some of the conditions violate the *Islām*ic teachings, they are automatically considered null and void. ʿĀ'ishah and Ibn ʿAbbās (رضي الله عنهم) reported that the Messenger (ﷺ) said:

«كل شرط ليس في كتاب الله فهو باطل، ولو كان مائة شرط.»

> **‹Every condition not according to the Book of Allāh is void, even if it be a hundred conditions.›** [2]

Abū Hurayrah (رضي الله عنه) reported that Allāh's Messenger (ﷺ) said:

«لا تسأل المرأةُ طلاقَ أختِها، لِتَسْتَفْرِغَ صحفتَها،
ولتنكحَ، فإن لها ما قُدِّرَ لها.»

> **‹Let not a woman require (as condition for marriage) the divorce of her sister (in *Islām*) in**

1 Recorded by al-Bayhaqī. Verified to be authentic by al-Albānī (*Irwā'ul-Ghalīl* no. 1893).

2 Recorded by al-Bukhārī, Muslim, and others.

order to take what is in her plate (of food) and marry (her husband). Indeed, she will only get what has been decreed for her.› [1]

Umm Mubashshir al-Anṣāriyyah (ﷺ) reported that after the death of her husband al-Barā' Bin Maʻrūr, Allāh's Messenger (ﷺ) said to her:

«إن زيدَ بن حارثةَ قد مات أهلُه، ولن آلو أن أختار له امرأةً، فقد اخترتُكِ له.»

‹Indeed, Zayd Bin Ḥārithah's wife has passed away, and I would like to find a wife for him; so I choose you for him.›

She was reluctant to accept and said, "I have promised my husband that I will not marry after him." The Prophet (ﷺ) replied, «إن هذا لا يصلح.» **‹This (condition) is not right.›** Then he asked her, «أترغبين عنه؟» **‹Do you dislike him?›** She said, "How can I dislike him when Allāh has placed him at such close position to you? It is only jealousy (that my late husband had). But, I will do whatever you say." So the Prophet (ﷺ) married her to Zayd and transferred her to live among his wives [2]. When a goat was milked and the milk brought to the Prophet (ﷺ), he would first give it Umm Mubashshir to drink before giving it to whomever he wished of his wives. One day, the Prophet (ﷺ) came into ʻĀ'ishah's house while she was with her. He put his hand on ʻĀ'ishah's knee and whispered something in her ear. She placed her hand over Allāh's Messenger (ﷺ) trying to push him away. Umm Mubashshir exclaimed, "How could you do this to Allāh's Messenger!" Allāh's Messenger (ﷺ) laughed and said:

«دعيها، فإنها تصنع هذا وأشدَّ من هذا.»

‹Leave her! She sometimes does this or even more

1 Recorded by al-Bukhārī and Abū Dāwūd.

2 That appears to be prior to the prohibition of adoption. Being the wife of his adopted son, the Prophet (ﷺ) treated Umm Mubashshir like a daughter-in-law.

than this.» [1]

The Contract

THE KHUṬBAH

It is recommended for the person conducting the marriage ceremony to start it with *khuṭbat ul-Ḥājah* that was reported by Ibn Mas'ūd and Jābir (﷽). [2]

ĪJĀB AND QABŪL

Ījāb and *qabūl* (offering and acceptance) are the main and actual pillars of the contract. They signify the mutual agreement and acceptance between the two parties to join in this marriage bond. *Ījāb* and *qabūl* must be stated in clear, well defined words, in one and the same sitting, and in the presence of the witnesses.

The person conducting the ceremony may help the two parties say the following (or something to the same effect):

a. **The *walī*:**

«أنكحتك موكِّلَتي (فلانة)

على شِرعةِ اللهِ (ﷻ) وسُنَّةِ رسولِهِ (ﷺ)،

وعلى الصِّداقِ والشّروطِ المسماةِ بيننا.»

"I offer you my principal (so-and-so) according to Allāh's (ﷻ) Law and His Messenger's (ﷺ) *Sunnah*, and for the *mahr* and conditions to which we have agreed."

b. **The bridegroom:**

---

1   Recorded by aṭ-Ṭabarānī and al-Bukhārī(in *at-Tārīkh*). Verified to be authentic by al-Albānī (*aṣ-Ṣaḥīḥah* no. 608).

2   This *khuṭbah* is fully cited at the beginning of the Prelude of this book.

«قبلتُ نِكاحَ موكِّلَتِك (فلانة)

على شِرعةِ اللّه (ﷻ) وسُنَّةِ رسولِه (ﷺ)،

وعلى الصِّداقِ والشّروطِ المسماةِ بيننا.»

"I accept marrying your principal (so-and-so) according to Allāh's (ﷻ) Law and His Messenger's (ﷺ) *Sunnah*, and for the *mahr* and conditions to which we have agreed."

The *ījāb* and *qabūl* must coincide in content. Any discrepancy between them would invalidate the contract. For example, if the *walī* says, "I give you my principal in marriage for a *mahr* of one-thousand," and the bridegroom responds by saying, "I accept marrying your principal for a *mahr* of eight hundred," the contract becomes immediately invalid.

Writing the Contract

Documenting the marriage contract is not a requirement for the contract's validity. However, it is important to document it for future reference and to preserve the rights of the husband and wife.

A sample marriage contract (or certificate) is included in the Appendix.

Outcome of the Marriage Contract

Once the marriage contract is executed, all rights and responsibilities for the two spouses, including the wife's advanced *mahr*, become immediately due. The details of this are covered in the third book of this series. [1]

---

1 See "The Fragile Vessels" by the author.

CHAPTER 5

CELEBRATING THE WEDDING

Publicizing the Marriage

A wedding marks the beginning of a new relationship between a man and woman who previously were strangers. Subsequently, the married couple might be seen in different places and, if the marriage was not publicized, some people may have ill thoughts about them. Because of this, it is important to make the marriage as public as possible — without going into extravagance and excess in doing that.

'Abdullāh Bin az-Zubayr (🙵) reported that the Messenger (🙵) said:

« أعلنوا النكاح. »

‹Announce the marriage.› [1]

As-Sā'ib Bin Yazīd (🙵) reported that Allāh's Messenger (🙵) said:

« أشيدوا النكاحَ وأعلنوه. »

‹Publicize the marriage and announce it.› [2]

Habbār Bin al-Aswad (🙵) reported that he gave one of his daughters in marriage. Allāh's Messenger (🙵) heard the noise (of celebrating the wedding) and inquired about it. He was told that Habbār married his daughter. So the Prophet (🙵) said:

« أشيدوا النّكاحَ، أشيدوا النّكاح. هذا النّكاحُ لا السّفاحَ. »

---

1 Recorded by Aḥmad, Ibn Ḥibbān, and others. Verified to be authentic by al-Albānī (*Ādāb uz-Zifāf* p. 183).

2 Recorded by aṭ-Ṭabarānī (in *al-Kabīr*) and others. Verified to be *hasan* by al-Albānī (*Ṣaḥīḥ ul-Jāmi'* no. 1010, 1011 & *aṣ-Ṣaḥīḥah* no. 1463).

‹**Publicize the marriage, publicize the marriage. This is a marriage, not fornication.**› [1]

Supplications

It is recommended to invoke blessings and prosperity for the married couple. Jābir (🙵) reported that the Messenger (🙵) made the following *duʻā* for him at his wedding:

«بارك الله لك.»

‹**May Allāh bless (your wife and marriage) for you.**› [2]

Buraydah Bin al-Ḥaṣīb (🙵) reported that a group of *al-Anṣār* told ʻAlī (🙵), "Why don't you consider Fāṭimah (for marriage)?" Acting upon their advice, he went to the Prophet (🙵) who asked him, «ما حاجةُ ابنِ أبي طالبٍ؟» ‹**What does the son of Abū Ṭālib need?**› He replied, "O Allāh's Messenger! I came in regard to Fāṭimah the daughter of Allāh's Messenger." The Messenger (🙵) replied, «مرحباً وأهلاً.» ‹***Marḥaban wa-ahlan*** — **Welcome, and a family member,**› [3] and he said no more. ʻAlī went back to that group of *al-Anṣār* who were waiting for him. They asked him, "What do you bring?" He said, "I do not know, except that he said to me, '*marḥaban wa-ahlan*.'" They said, "Just one of these two words would suffice you from Allāh's Messenger (🙵); he offered you the 'family' and 'vastness'." Later on, after the Prophet (🙵) married Fāṭimah to ʻAlī, he told him:

---

1   Recorded by Ibn Mandah. Verified to be authentic by al-Albānī (*aṣ-Ṣaḥīḥah* no. 1463).

2   Recorded by al-Bukhārī, Muslim, and others. A more complete version of this *ḥadīth* was cited in Chapter 2.

3   These two words are commonly used to welcome a guest. The first literary meaning, "Your presence is a cause of ease and vastness." The second means, "You are like a member of the family."

«إنه لا بد للعرس (للعروس) من وليمة.»

‹Indeed, a wedding (or a bridegroom) must have a *walīmah*.›

So Saʿd said, "I will bring a ram." And another man said, "I will bring so much of corn." Then, when it was his wedding night, the Prophet (ﷺ) told ʿAlī, «لا تُحدِثْ شيئاً حتى تلقاني.» **‹Do not do anything until you meet me.›** So the Prophet (ﷺ) went over to ʿAlī, asked for some water, performed *wuḍūʾ* with it, poured it over ʿAlī, and said:

«اللهم بارك فيهما، وبارك لهما في بنائهما.»

‹O Allāh, bless them and bless their wedding for them.› [1]

ʿĀʾishah (رضي الله عنها) reported that when Allāh's Messenger (ﷺ) married her, her mother took her into his house for her wedding night, and she saw there some women from *al-Anṣār* who congratulated her, saying:

"على الخيرِ والبَركة، وعلى خير طائر."

"(May your marriage be) good and blessed, and may you have the best fortune." [2]

Abū Hurayrah (رضي الله عنه) reported that Allāh's Messenger (ﷺ) used to congratulate newly-wed people, saying:

«بارَكَ الله لك، وبارك عليك، وجمع بينكما في خير.»

‹May Allāh bless (her) for you, and bless you (for her) and keep you together in prosperity.› [3]

---

1 Recorded by Ibn Saʿd, aṭ-Ṭabarānī, and Ibn ʿAsākir. Verified to be *ḥasan* by al-Albānī (*Ādāb uz-Zifāf* pp. 173-174).

2 Recorded by al-Bukhārī, Muslim, and others.

3 Recorded by Abū Dāwūd, at-Tirmiḏhī, and others. Verified to be authentic by al-Albānī (*Ādāb uz-Zifāf* p. 175).

ʿAqīl Bin Abī Ṭālib (ﷺ) reported that the Messenger (ﷺ) taught them to say this *duʿā* (for newly-wed people):

«بارك الله لكم، وبارك عليكم.»

‹May Allāh bless (your marriage and wife) for you and bless you.› [1]

Singing and Beating on the *Duff*

A Recommended Act

As part of celebrating a wedding, it is recommended to sing and beat on the *duff*. The *duff* is a musical instrument similar to a tambourine, but without rings.

Abū Balj Yaḥyā Bin Salīm reported that he said to Muḥammad Bin Ḥāṭib (ﷺ), "I married two wives, and in neither of the two weddings was there a sound (of *duff*)." Muḥammad then told him that Allāh's Messenger (ﷺ) said:

«فصل ما بين الحلال والحرام ضرب الدفّ والصوتُ في النكاح.»

‹What distinguishes between the lawful (i.e. marriage) and the prohibited (i.e., adultery) is beating the *duff* and the sound (of singing) at wedding.› [2]

ʿĀʾishah (ﷺ) reported that she prepared a bride for her wedding to a man from the *Anṣār*. Allāh's Messenger (ﷺ) said:

«يا عائشة، ما كان معكم لهو، فإن الأنصار يعجبهم اللهو؟»

---

1 Recorded by an-Nasāʾī, Ibn Mājah, and others. Verified to be *ḥasan* by al-Albānī (*Ādāb uz-Zifāf* pp. 175-177).

2 Recorded by an-Nasāʾī, at-Tirmiḏẖī, and others. Verified to be *ḥasan* by al-Albānī (*Ādāb uz-Zifāf* p. 183, *Ṣaḥīḥ ul-Jāmiʿ* no. 4206, *Irwāʾ ul-Ghalīl* no. 1994).

‹O ʻĀʼishah, did you not have some singing? Indeed, the *Anṣār* like singing.› [1]

WHAT TO SING

Singing should be done using simple and innocent wording, avoiding corrupt songs that call to sinning and disobedience.

In another report fromʻĀʼishah (ﷺ), the Prophet (ﷺ) said:

«فهل بعثتم معها جاريةً تضرب بالدف وتغني؟»

‹Shouldn't you have sent with the bride a little girl to beat on the *duff* and sing?›

ʻĀʼishah (ﷺ) asked, "What would she say?" He (ﷺ) replied:

«أتيناكم أتيناكم   فحيونا نحييكم
لولا الذهب الأحمـ   ـر ما حلت بواديكم
لولا الحنطة السمرا   ء ما سمنت عذاريكم»

‹We came to you, we came to you.
So greet us, and we will greet you.
Had it not been for the red gold,
Your desert-land would not have been inhabited.
And had it not been for the dark grain,
Your virgin girls would not have gained weight.› [2]

WHO PERFORMS THE SINGING AND BEATING

We see from the above reports that singing and *duff*-beating is performed by women, among women, and for women only. No men are to be involved in any of that. Thus, today's practice during weddings where men sing, play music, and dance is in discord with the

1 Recorded by al-Bukhārī and others.

2 Recorded by aṭ-Ṭabarānī and others. Verified to be *ḥasan* by al-Albānī (*Irwāʼ ul-Ghalīl* no. 1995 & *Ādāb uz-Zifāf* p. 181).

Sunnah. A man should be loathsome to do such effeminate acts.

A WORD ABOUT MUSIC

Some people may conclude from the above that music is permissible in *Islām*. That would be a wrong conclusion conflicting with the authentic texts and the consensus of the early scholars of *Islām*, including the Four *Imāms*.

Anas, ʿImrān, Abū Umāmah, ʿAlī, and Abū Hurayrah (ﷺ) reported that Allāh's Messenger (ﷺ) said:

«ليكوننّ في هذه الأمةِ خسفٌ وقذفٌ ومسخ، وذلك إذا شربوا الخمور، واتخذوا القيناتِ، وضربوا بالمعازف.»

‹There will be among (the people of) this *Ummah* earth-collapse, stoning, and metamorphosis. That will be when they drink alcoholic beverages, keep female singers, and play on musical instruments.› [1]

Musical instruments are prohibited in *Islām*. The only exception to that is the *duff*, and only after fulfilling three conditions:

1. It should be a *duff* without rings.
2. It may only be used during *ʿīd* and wedding celebrations.
3. It may only be used by women.

The *Walīmah*

The *walīmah* is an important part of celebrating a wedding, and is be discussed in detail in Chapter 7.

1 Recorded by Aḥmad, at-Tirmiṯẖī, and others. Verified to be authentic by al-Albānī (*Ṣaḥīḥ ul-Jāmiʿ* no. 5467 & *aṣ-Ṣaḥīḥah* no. 2203).

Giving Presents

Giving presents is a good practice in all occasions. The presents should be given without extravagance or show-off. Also, they should not be given with the understanding that it is an obligatory practice associated with a wedding.

Abū Hurayrah (🙵) reported that Allāh's Messenger (🙵) said:

«تهادُوا تحابُّوا.»

‹**Exchange presents: that will make you love each other.**› [1]

Anas Bin Mālik (🙵) reported that when the Prophet (🙵) married Zaynab (🙵), Umm Sulaym [2] told Anas, "Let us give a present to Allāh's Messenger (🙵)." Anas agreed, "Yes, do." So she brought dates, butter, and dried yogurt, put them in a pot, and turned them into a smooth mixture (called *ḥaysah* or *ḥays*). When Anas took the pot to the Prophet (🙵), he told him to set it down and then go and invite a certain number of men, as well as anyone whom he met along the way. Anas did as he was commanded, and by the time he was back he found the house overflowing with people. The Prophet (🙵) put his hands over the *ḥaysah*, read over it as much as Allāh willed, then invited the people to eat of it, ten after ten. He told them:

«أذكروا آسم الله، وليأكل كل رجلٍ مما يليه.»

‹**Utter Allāh's name, and let each man eat from his side.**›

Thus, all those who were present ate from that food. [3]

---

1   Recorded by Abū Yaʻlā, al-Bayhaqī and al-Bukhārī in *al-Adab ul-Mufrad*. Verified to be *ḥasan* by al-Albānī (*Irwāʼ ul-Ghalīl* no. 1601).

2   Anas's mother.

3   Recorded by al-Bukhārī, Muslim, and others.

Sinning during Celebrations

There are many sins and acts of disobedience frequently practiced by large numbers of Muslims during wedding celebrations. They think that a wedding is an occasion on which one may abandon some of his *Islām*ic principles.

In the rest of this section, we highlight a few such acts of disobedience, hoping by that to warn the Muslims against participating in any of them. For more details on some of the following topics, one is referred to "Celebrations in Islām" by the author.

Mingling of Sexes

One of the frequently practiced acts of disobedience is for women to mingle with men who are not their *maḥram*s. Together, they would then do things prohibited in *Islām*, such as:

- Touching and shaking hands.
- Men and woman chatting, laughing, and sometimes flirting with each other.
- Men and women staring at each other.

All of this is prohibited and leads to major harms for the individual and the Muslim society, as is discussed in detail in the second part of this series.

Playing Music and Drinking Alcohol

Unfortunately, most Muslims play music or listen to it during wedding celebrations. They often associate this with drinking, or with "national" or belly dancing, all in the name of *Islām*!

All of this is prohibited, and constitutes great sinning that makes one liable to a severe punishment from Allāh (ﷻ).

Abū ʿĀmir and Abū Mālik al-Ashʿarī (رضي الله عنهما) reported that Allāh's Messenger (ﷺ) said:

«لَيَكونَنَّ مِن أمّتي أقوامٌ يستحلّون الحِرَ والحريرَ والخمرَ والمعازفَ،

ولينزلنَّ أقوامٌ إلى جنب عَلَم، يروح عليهم برائحةٍ لهم، يأتيهم لحاجةٍ فيقولون ٱرجع إلينا غداً، فيُبيِّتُهم اللّهُ ويضع العلم، ويمسخُ آخرينَ قردةً وخنازيرَ إلى يوم القيامة.»

‹There will be among my *Ummah* those who will indulge in *ḥir* [1], wearing silk [2], *khamr*, and musical instruments. Some of those people will camp beside a mountain. A poor shepherd tending their cattle will come to them in the evening asking for some (financial) help. They will say, "Come back tomorrow." So Allāh will destroy most of them during the night, bringing the mountain down over them, and will transform the rest to apes and pigs until the Day of Resurrection.› [3]

IMPROPER APPEARANCE

It is recommended for Muslims to dress up for celebrations. In doing so, however, both men and women often commit many violations to *Islām*, among which are the following:

- The women expose their heads, arms, legs, and other parts of their bodies.
- The women wear perfumes, makeup, decorated and alluring clothing, and some national costumes that contradict the *Islām*ic teachings.
- The women imitate the disbelieving women in their hairdos, in keeping long nails and covering them with nail polish, etc.
- The men wear natural silk (rarely nowadays) or gold (more often).
- The men wear tight pants and non-*Islām*ic attires (such as cowboy hats, tuxedos, etc).

---

1 Adultery and fornications.

2 Wearing natural silk is prohibited for men.

3 Recorded by al-Bukhārī without *isnād* (no. 5590), but connected in four different ways by Abū Dāwūd and others. Verified to be authentic by Ibn Ḥajar, al-Albānī (*Ṣaḥīḥ ul-Jāmiʿ* no. 5466 & *aṣ-Ṣaḥīḥah* no. 91), and others.

- The men shave their beards, wear bracelets or necklaces (or neck-chains), and do other things that constitute imitation of women.

EXTRAVAGANCE

People often spend extravagantly during wedding celebrations. They turn their weddings into fierce arenas for showoff. They waste money on things that are of no benefit for the Muslims, such as the following:

- Holding the weddings in expensive hotels and ballrooms where lavish foods are served and many violations to *Islām* are committed.
- Distributing to the attendees expensive artifacts filled with sweets.
- Throwing silver or golden coins for the lucky people to catch.

Allāh (ﷻ) says:

﴿ولا تُبَذِّرْ تَبْذِيرًا ۝ إِنَّ ٱلْمُبَذِّرِينَ كَانُوٓا۟ إِخْوَٰنَ ٱلشَّيَٰطِينِ، وَكَانَ ٱلشَّيْطَٰنُ لِرَبِّهِۦ كَفُورًا ۝﴾ الإسراء ٢٦-٢٧

«Do not waste your wealth senselessly. Those who spend wastefully are the brothers of the devils; and the Devil is ever ungrateful to his Lord.» [1]

More about this is covered under the discussion of the *walīmah* (Chapter 7).

TAKING PICTURES

A common modern practice during wedding celebrations is taking large numbers of pictures (or videotaping) of the newly-wed couple, their relatives, and their other guests. Those pictures usually show the women exposing their heads and other parts of their bodies and making various poses with men who are not their *maḥrams*.

A Muslim should not take a picture or help in taking it unless it

---

1 *Al-Isrā'* 17:26-27.

fulfills a need that cannot be fulfilled otherwise. What we sadly observe is that many Muslims, in addition to taking pictures for which there is no necessity or need, they take pictures that reflect a great amount of sinning and disobedience! Thus, they "freeze" their sinning, so that they and other people would see for many years to come, in addition to adding to their balance of evil deeds on the Day of Judgement.

'Ā'ishah (ﷺ) reported that Allāh's Messenger (ﷺ) once entered when she had a curtain covering an alcove in her house. The curtain had some pictures drawn on it. When the Prophet (ﷺ) saw it, his face showed anger and he said:

«إن الذين يصنعون هذه الصور يُعذَّبون يوم القيامة،
ويُقال لهم أحيوا ما خلقتم.»

‹Indeed, those who make these pictures will be tortured on the Day of Resurrection and will be told, "Give life to what you have created."›

So she removed the curtain, cut it, and made pillows with it. [1]

Ibn Mas'ūd reported that Allāh's Messenger (ﷺ) said:

«إن أشد الناس عذاباً يوم القيامة المصوِّرون.»

‹Indeed, the people who will receive the most severe punishment on the Day of Resurrection are those who make pictures.› [2]

Abū Ṭalḥah, 'Alī, and others (ﷺ) reported that Allāh's Messenger (ﷺ) said:

«إن الملائكة لا تدخل بيتاً فيه كلبٌ أو صورة.»

‹Indeed, the angels do not enter a house in which

1 Recorded by al-Bukhārī, Muslim, and others.

2 Recorded by Muslim, Aḥmad, and others.

there is a dog or a picture.› [1]

Imitation of the Disbelievers

Some Muslims imitate the disbelievers in many aspects of their wedding celebrations, such as:

- Mailing formal wedding invitation-cards tailored according to the ways of the *kuffār*.
- Holding "bachelor", and "bachelorette" parties for the bridegroom and bride in which major sins are committed.
- Holding a bridal-shower in which the attendees are required to bring gifts to the bride.
- The bride wearing a special expensive white wedding gown which usually exposes generous portions of her physique.
- The newly-wed couple wearing wedding rings to indicate their new "married" status. Unfortunately, this and the previous wrong practices are now so widely spread among the Muslims, all over the world, that they are commonly thought as being integral parts an *Islām*ic wedding!

Other Violations

There are many other violations commonly committed during wedding celebrations. We will conclude by just a few of them:

- Admitting the bridegroom, sometimes accompanied by other men, into the women's section of the wedding in order to meet his bride and kiss her in front of a large number of women, many of them improperly dressed. This is a shameless act that has no basis or support in *Islām*.
- Missing a number of *jamā'ah* prayers for the sake of the wedding.

---

1 Recorded by al-Bukhārī, Muslim, and others.

CHAPTER 6

CONSUMMATING THE MARRIAGE

Advising the Married Couple

Prior to leaving the married couple alone on their wedding night, it is important to give them some advice in regard to the *Islām*ic guidelines for marital intimacy and other issues of importance for a newly-wed couple. Advising the bride is usually done by her mother. Most of what needs to be said is covered in this chapter or the rest of this book and its two other companions [1].

Kindness To the Bride

The husband should be extremely kind to his bride on their first night together, especially if she is a virgin. He should understand that this night marks the beginning of a totally new life for her. This would usually make her nervous and slow in cooperating with him.

Thus, he should not immediately force himself on her. He should understand that if she does not appear to be fully ready on the first night, he can work on easing down her emotions while waiting for the ultimate union between them one or more days later — as might be necessary.

Allāh's Messenger (ﷺ) was very kind and gentle with 'Ā'ishah (رضي الله عنها) on her first night with him. He gave her some milk to drink, allowed her friends to remain with her for a while, and talked to them jokingly — all of which was meant to make her feel at ease.

Asmā' Bint Yazīd Bin as-Sakan [2] reported that she adorned

---

1 See "Closer Than a Garment" and "The Fragile Vessels" by the author.

2 She was Mu'<u>th</u> Bin Jabal's cousin: one of the *Anṣār* women who gave her covenant to the Prophet (ﷺ) during Bay'at ur-Riḍwān. She lived until the time of Yazīd Bin Mu'āwiyah.

'Ā'ishah (رضي الله عنها) for the Prophet (ﷺ) and then invited him to come and see her. He came and sat next to her. He was given a large cup of milk. He drank some of it and then gave it to her. She shyly lowered her head, and Asmā' scolded her saying, "Do not reject Allāh's Messenger's offer." So she took the cup and drank some. The Prophet (ﷺ) then told her, «أعطي تربك.» ‹Give your friend.› Asmā' said, "O Allāh's Messenger! First take it back and drink from it, then give it to me with your hand." He took it, drank from it, and then gave it to her. She sat down, put it on her knees, and turned it around until she had her lips on the spot where the Prophet (ﷺ) drank [1]. Then he pointed to some other women who were with her and said, «ناولي صواحبك.» ‹Give your friends.› They said, "We have no desire for it." He said:

«لا تجمعنَ جوعاً وكذباً.»

‹Do not combine hunger with lying.› [2]

Praying Two *Rak'ah*s Together

It is recommended for the newly-wed couple to pray two *rak'āt* in *jamā'ah*, with the groom leading the prayer. This would be a great indication that, from their first night, they meet together on an act of obedience to Allāh (ﷻ).

Abū Sa'īd, the *mawlā* (freed slave) of Abū Usayd, reported that while he was still a slave, he got married. He invited a number of the Prophet's (ﷺ) companions to his wedding, including Ibn Mas'ūd, Huthayfah, and Abū Tharr (رضي الله عنهم). While they were there, the *iqāmah* was given for the prayer, and Abū Tharr advanced to lead them. They all told him, "Hold off (because the host has the right to lead)." He asked, "Is that so?" They said, "Yes." Thus, Abū Sa'īd advanced and led them in the prayer, even though he was an owned slave. After the prayer, they taught him:

---

1   Seeking the blessing from Allāh's Messenger's (ﷺ) touch.

2   Recorded by Aḥmad. Verified to be *ḥasan* by al-Albānī (*Ādāb uz-Zifāf* p. 92).

"When your bride enters to your presence, pray two *rak'ah*s (with her), then ask Allāh to grant you of her good and protect you from her evil, and then you are free to do what you want with your bride." [1]

Shaqīq reported that a man called Ḥarīz came to 'Abdullāh Bin Mas'ūd and said, "I have just married a young virgin, and I fear that she might dislike me." Ibn Mas'ūd (⬥) said:

"Indeed, love (between the spouses) is from Allāh, and dislike is from Satan who wants to make you dislike what Allāh made lawful to you. When she comes to you, tell her to pray two *rak'āt* behind you. Then say:

"اللهم بارِك لي في أهلي، وبارِك لهم فيَّ. اللهم أَجمع بيننا ما جمعتَ بخير، وفرِّق بيننا إذا فرَّقتَ إلى خير."

'Allāhumma bārik lī fī ahlī, wa-bārik lahum fiyya. Allāhumm ajma' baynanā ma jama'ta bikhayr, wa-farriq baynanā ithā farraqta ilā khayr — O Allāh, bless my wife for me, and bless me for her. O Allāh, let our get-together be upon what is good, and let our separation, when you separate between us, be to what is good.'" [2]

Invoking Allāh's Blessing

After praying the two *rak'āt* together, it is recommended for the husband to make supplications and invoke Allāh's blessings on himself and his bride.

'Abdullāh Bin 'Amr (⬥) reported that Allāh's Messenger (⬥)

---

1   Recorded by Ibn Abī Shaybah and 'Abd ur-Razzāq. Verified to be authentic by al-Albānī (*Ādāb uz-Zifāf* p. 94).

2   Recorded by Ibn Abī Shaybah and 'Abd ur-Razzāq. Verified to be authentic by al-Albānī (*Ādāb uz-Zifāf* p. 96).

said:

«إذا أفاد أحدُكم امرأةً أو خادماً أو دابّة فليأخذ بناصيتها،
وليسم اللّه، وليدع بالبركة، وليقل: "بسم الله، اللهم بارك
لي فيها. اللهم إني أسألك من خيرِها وخيرِ ما جبلتَها عليه،
وأعوذ بكَ من شرِّها وشرِّ ماجبلتَها عليه." وإن كان بعيراً
فليأخذ بذروة سنامه.»

‹When one of you acquires a wife, a servant, or a riding animal, he should hold her (or it) by the forehead, invoke Allāh's blessing, and say: "*Bismillāh, allāhumma bārik lī fīhā. Allāhumma innī as'aluka min khayrihā wa-khayri mā jabaltahā 'alayhi, wa-a'ūthu bika min sharrihā wa-sharri mā jabaltahā 'alayh* — With Allāh's name. O Allāh, bless her for me. O Allāh, I ask You to grant me of her (or its) good, and the good upon which You created her (or it); and I ask You to protect me from her (or its) evil and any evil upon which You created her (or it)." And if it is a camel (that he acquires), one should hold it by the peak of its hump (and say the same).› [1]

*Islām*ic Etiquettes of Marital Intimacy

There are many guidelines that one should keep in mind when he (or she) is ready to intimately approach his (or her) spouse. In what follows, we briefly cover a few of them. A detailed coverage of this subject is included in the second book of this series [2].

---

1 A combined report recorded by al-Bukhārī, Ibn Abī Shaybah, and others.

2 See "Closer Than a Garment" by the author.

Supplication Before Intercourse

Even at the peak of his passion, a believer does not forget his Lord (ﷻ). He remembers that his intercourse with his wife is a means of fulfilling many noble purposes — not only his lust (see Chapter 1 in this regard). One of those noble purposes is producing a good progeny. Thus, it is important to supplicate to Allāh asking him to keep Satan away from him and his progeny.

Ibn ʿAbbās (ﷺ) reported that the Messenger (ﷺ) said:

«لو أن أحدكم إذا أراد أن يأتيَ أهلهُ قال: "بسم اللّه، اللّهم جنِّبنا الشيطانَ، وجنّب الشيطانَ ما رزقتنا،" فإنه إن قُضيَ بينهما ولدٌ من ذلك لم يضرّه الشيطانُ أبداً.»

‹When one of you wants to approach his wife, if he says:
"*Bismillāh. Allāhumma jannib nash-Shayṭān, wa-jannib ish-Shayṭāna mā razaqtanā* —
With the Name of Allāh. O Allāh, keep Satan away from us, and keep him away from what You grant us,"
If it is then decreed that they get a child (from that approach), Satan will never harm it.› [1]

Miscellaneous *Ādāb* for Intercourse

The following is a list of additional important *ādāb* that one should observe when being intimate or having intercourse with one's spouse.

1. The man may only have intercourse with his wife in her front entry (vagina). Approaching her from the back entry is a major sin.

2. During his wife's menses, a man may not have intercourse with her, but may otherwise enjoy other parts of her body. Performing intercourse with a menstruating woman is a major sin.

---

1 Recorded by al-Bukhārī, Muslim, and others.

3. A person (man or woman) becomes *junub* (unclean) in one of two ways:

    a) By climaxing and ejaculation, which results from intercourse, wet dreams, foreplay, etc.

    b) By performing intercourse — regardless of whether it results in ejaculation or not.

4. A *junub* person must take a *ghusl* (bath) before being able to pray. It is further recommended for a *junub* to take the *ghusl* before going to sleep or mentioning Allāh. If that is not possible, one should at least wash his (or her) private parts and perform a *wuḍū'*.

5. It is strongly prohibited for the two spouses to disclose to other people the secrets and happenings that take place during their intimacy sessions.

The Morning Following the Wedding

On the morning following the wedding night, it is recommended for the husband to go out to his family members and relatives, greet them, and supplicate for them.

Anas (🙽) reported:

> "When Allāh's Messenger (🙽) had his wedding with Zaynab, he offered a *walīmah* in which the Muslims ate their fill of bread and meat. Then (in the morning) he went out to the Mothers of the Believers, gave them *salām*, and supplicated for them. In return, they gave him *salām* and supplicated for him. Thus he used to do on the morning following his wedding." [1]

---

1   Recorded by an-Nasā'ī and Ibn Saʻd. Verified to be authentic by al-Albānī (*Ādāb uz-Zifāf* pp. 138-137).

Honeymoon

One of the common practices right after a wedding is for the newlywed couple to go on a "honeymoon" trip. Depending on the couple's finances, that trip would usually be to a country or area that has some attraction for tourism.

There is no doubt that the honeymoon is a practice of the non-Muslims, in which many Muslims have rushed to imitate them — just as they do in many other respects of their lives.

Furthermore, a honeymoon is usually an occasion for adding to one's record of sins: it involves mixing with many disbelievers, listening to music, going to restaurants where alcohol is served, going to beaches and other attractions where the people are improperly attired, and so on.

If one gets a few days off from work on the occasion of his wedding, he should not use these days in disobeying Allāh. Rather, he can take the chance to go with his bride on a trip of *ʿUmrah* or for visiting some family members to preserve the kinship ties and invite them to the good teachings of *Islām*.

CHAPTER 7

THE *WALĪMAH*

Definition and Ruling

The *walīmah* (or wedding feast) is a meal offered by the husband to the friends and family after the consummation of the marriage.

The *walīmah* is *wājib* (obligatory) upon the husband. Buraydah Bin al-Ḥaṣīb (ﷺ) reported that when ʿAlī (ﷺ) married Fāṭimah, Allāh's Messenger (ﷺ) said:

«إنه لا بد للعرس (للعروس) من وليمة.»

‹Indeed, a wedding (or a bridegroom) must have a *walīmah*.›

So Saʿd said, "I will bring a ram." And another man said, "I will bring so much of corn." [1]

When ʿAbd ur-Raḥmān Bin ʿAwf (ﷺ) migrated to al-Madīnah, the Prophet (ﷺ) made him brother [2] with Saʿd Bin ar-Rabīʿ al-Anṣārī. Saʿd (ﷺ) was a wealthy man. He took ʿAbd ur-Raḥmān to his home where they ate, then he said to him, "My brother! I am the wealthiest man of al-Madīnah, so I will divide my wealth in half between us; and I have two wives while you are my brother and you have no wife, so see which one of my two wives you like more and I will divorce her for you so that you would marry her after she concludes her *ʿiddah*."

---

1 Recorded by Aḥmad and an-Nasāʾī. Verified to be authentic by al-Albānī (*Ṣaḥīḥ ul-Jāmiʿ* no. 2419 & *Ādāb uz-Zifāf* pp. 144-145).

2 In the early years of *Hijrah*, the Prophet (ﷺ) used to pair the Muslims as brothers, with one of the pair from among the *Muhājirīn* and one from among the *Anṣār*. The *Anṣār*, being the original residents of al-Madīnah, were ready and willing to take upon themselves the burden of their brothers from Makkah who had left everything behind them when they made *Hijrah*.

ʿAbd ur-Raḥmān replied, "By Allāh no! May Allāh bless your family and wealth for you. Just show me the way to the market." He was shown the way to the market, and he traded and made profit. Soon after that, he came home with some *aqiṭ* (dried yogurt) and butter (as profit).

A while after that, the Prophet (ﷺ) saw ʿAbd ur-Raḥmān wearing yellowish garments (which were commonly worn by the newly wed). He (ﷺ) asked him, «مَهْيَمْ؟» **‹What has happened?›** He replied, "I have married a woman from the *Anṣār*." He (ﷺ) asked him, «ما سُقت إليها.» **‹What did you give her (as *mahr*)?›** He replied, "A date stone's weight of gold." The Prophet (ﷺ) then said:

«فبارَكَ اللّهُ لك. أولِمْ، ولو بشاة.»

> **‹May Allāh bless it for you. Offer a *walīmah* — even if it be with only one goat.›**

ʿAbd ur-Raḥmān concluded, "It then came to that, should I raise a stone, I would expect to find gold or silver underneath it (by virtue of the Prophet's (ﷺ) supplication)."

Anas (رضي الله عنه) concluded, "After ʿAbd ur-Raḥmān passed away, each one of his wives got a share of one-hundred-thousand *dīnārs*." [1]

Regulations and Recommendations

In addition to being obligatory, the following regulations apply to the *walīmah*.

TIME

Following the Prophet's (ﷺ) practice, the *walīmah* should normally be held on the wedding night or within the first three days following it.

Anas (رضي الله عنه) reported:

> "Allāh's Messenger (ﷺ) once consummated his

1 Recorded by al-Bukhārī, Muslim, and others.

marriage with one of his wives, so he sent me and I invited some men for food." [1]

Anas (⚕) also reported:

"The Prophet (⚕) married Ṣafiyyah and, as *mahr*, he granted her freedom. And he held the *walīmah* for three days." [2]

In a similar report, Anas (⚕) said:

"The Prophet (⚕) camped between Khaybar and al-Madīnah for three nights, consummating his marriage with Ṣafiyyah. I invited the Muslims to his *walīmah*, and it had no bread or meat. Leather sheets were spread on the ground, and dates and *aqiṭ* (dried yogurt) and butter were tossed over them, and the people ate their fill." [3]

And Anas (⚕) reported:

"When Allāh's Messenger (⚕) had his wedding with Zaynab, he offered a *walīmah* in which the Muslims ate their fill of bread and meat. Then (in the morning) he went out to the Mothers of the Believers, gave them *salām*, and supplicated for them. In return, they gave him *salām* and supplicated for him. Thus, he used to do that on the morning following his wedding." [4]

---

1   Recorded by al-Bukhārī and al-Bayhaqī.
2   Recorded by Abū Ya‘lā. Verified to be *ḥasan* by al-Albānī (*Ādāb uz-Zifāf* p. 146).
3   Recorded by al-Bukhārī, Muslim, and others.
4   Recorded by an-Nasā'ī and Ibn Sa‘d. Verified to be authentic by al-Albānī (*Ādāb uz-Zifāf* pp. 138-137).

TYPES OF FOOD

We conclude from the above reports about 'Alī and 'Abd ur-Raḥmān Bin 'Awf that it is recommended to include meat in a *walīmah*, with a minimum of one sheep or goat — if that is affordable.

Anas (☖) reported:

"ما رأيت رسول اللّه أَوْلَمَ على امرأةٍ من نسائه أَكثرَ أو أفضلَ

مما أولمَ على زينبَ، فإنه ذبح شاةً، وأطعمهم خبزاً ولحماً حتى تركوه. "

> "I never saw Allāh's Messenger (☖) offer as much food in any of his wives's *walīmah*s as he did in Zaynab's. He slaughtered a goat and fed the people bread and meat until they were full." [1]

However, meat is not a condition for a *walīmah*. We saw above (and will see again below) that the Prophet's (☖) *walīmah* when he married Ṣafiyyah did not include any meat.

HELPING WITH THE COST

The *walīmah* is the husband's obligation. However, it is permissible for other Muslims to help him in its cost or preparation. We have seen above that a number of Muslims helped 'Alī in preparing his *walīmah*. Similarly, Anas (☖) mentioned some more about the Prophet's (☖) marriage with Ṣafiyyah (☖) in the following:

> "While we were on our way (from Khaybar to al-Madīnah), Umm Sulaym prepared Ṣafiyyah for the Prophet (☖) and presented her to him during the night. On the following morning, after the Prophet (☖) had consummated his marriage, he said:

«من كان عنده فضل زاد فليجئْ به»

‹**Whoever has any extra provision, let him bring it to**

---

1   Recorded by al-Bukhārī, Muslim, and others.

us.›

Leather sheets were laid down. Some men brought *aqiṭ*, others dates, and others butter. They made *ḥays* (name of a dish) from those items. And the people ate of that *ḥays* and drank from rain water that gathered in basins next to them. Thus was Allāh's Messenger's (ﷺ) *walīmah*." [1]

WHOM TO INVITE

One should invite to the *walīmah* his Muslim relatives, friends, and acquaintances, especially the righteous among them. Abū Saʿīd al-Khudrī (ﷺ) reported that Allāh's Messenger (ﷺ) said:

«لا تصاحب إلا مؤمناً ولا يأكل طعامك إلا تقي.»

‹Do not accompany except a believer, and do not feed your food except to a pious person.›

As much as possible, sinful people and disbelievers should be excluded from the invitation — unless there appears to be a strong chance that they would be subjected to *daʿwah*, and that their presence would not influence the attendees in a negative way.

In inviting to a *walīmah*, one should not distinguish between the poor and rich. Abū Hurayrah (ﷺ) reported that the Messenger (ﷺ) said:

«شر الطعام طعام الوليمة، يُدعى لها الأغنياء، ويُمنعُها المساكين، ومن لم يجب الدعوة فقد عصى الله ورسوله.»

‹The worst food is that of a *walīmah* to which the rich are invited but the poor are not. And he who rejects the invitation (to a *walīmah*) has surely disobeyed Allāh and His Messenger.› [2]

---

1 Recorded by al-Bukhārī, Muslim, and others.

2 Recorded by Muslim and others from Abū Hurayrah, Ibn ʿAbbās, and Ibn

In another report from Abū Hurayrah, Allāh's Messenger (ﷺ) said:

«شر الطعام طعامُ الوليمة يُمنعُها من يأتيها، ويُدعى إليها من يأباها. ومن لم يجب الدعوة فقد عصى اللّه ورسولَه.»

‹The worst of food is that of a *walīmah* to which those who come (because of hunger) are turned away, and those who are invited do not wish to attend (because they have no need for food). And he who does not answer the invitation (to a *walīmah*) has surely disobeyed Allāh and His Messenger.› [1]

Manners for the Host

There are certain *ādāb* that should be implemented by a host when he invites people to a wedding *walīmah* or any other meal. Some of them have been included in the previous section. In what follows we include some additional important *ādāb*.

SINCERITY

One should realize and remember that feeding is an act of worship. Thus it should be performed with sincerity — only seeking Allāh's reward for it.

ʿAbdullāh Bin ʿAmr Bin al-ʿĀṣ (ﷺ) reported that a man asked Allāh's Messenger (ﷺ), "What acts are superior in *Islām*?" He (ﷺ) replied:

«تطعمُ الطعام، وتَقرأُ السلامَ على من عرفتَ ومن لم تعرِفْ.»

‹It is to feed the food (to the people), and greet with

ʿUmar. Some of the reports in al-Bukhārī and Muslim indicate that this is *mawqūf*, being the saying of Abū Hurayrah. But other authentic reports prove that it is stated by the Prophet (ﷺ) (see *Irwāʾ ul-Ghalīl* no. 1947 and *aṣ-Ṣaḥīḥah* no. 1085).

1 Recorded by al-Bukhārī, Muslim, and others. See the previous footnote.

***salām* those whom you know and those whom you do not.›** [1]

Ṣuhayb (ﷺ) reported that Allāh's Messenger (ﷺ) said:

«خيركم من أطعم الطعامَ ورد السلام.»

‹The best among you are those who feed the food (to others) and respond to the *salām*.› [2]

AVOIDING EXTRAVAGANCE AND SHOW-OFF

Some people like to impress others by their wealth and status through being extravagant and wasteful in holding banquets, receptions, or other occasions. They invite their guests to expensive hotels and offer them costly food and services, all of which are often beyond their means and extremely straining to their resources for a long time to follow.

All of that is prohibited, and constitutes clear defiance to Allāh's limits. Allāh (ﷻ) says:

﴿ولَا تُبَذِّرْ تَبْذِيرًا ۝ إِنَّ ٱلْمُبَذِّرِينَ كَانُوٓاْ إِخْوَانَ ٱلشَّيَاطِينِ، وَكَانَ ٱلشَّيْطَانُ لِرَبِّهِۦ كَفُورًا ۝﴾ الإسراء ٢٦-٢٧

«And do not spend wastefully: Indeed the wasteful are brothers of the devils, and the Devil has ever been ungrateful to his Lord.» [3]

And Allāh (ﷻ) says:

﴿وكُلُواْ وَٱشْرَبُواْ وَلَا تُسْرِفُوٓاْ، إِنَّهُۥ لَا يُحِبُّ ٱلْمُسْرِفِينَ ۝﴾ الأعراف ٣١

«Eat and drink, but do not be excessive; verily, He

---

1 Recorded by al-Bukhārī and Muslim.

2 Recorded by Aḥmad, al-Ḥākim, and others. Verified to be *ḥasan* by al-Albānī (*Ṣaḥīḥ ul-Jāmiʿ* no. 3318).

3 *Al-Isrāʾ* 17:26-27.

does not like the extravagant.» [1]

Al-Mughīrah Bin Shuʿbah (ﷺ) reported that Allāh's Messenger (ﷺ) said:

«إنَّ اللّه كره لكم ثلاثاً، قيل وقال، وإضاعة المال، وكثرة السؤال»

‹Allāh verily hates three qualities for you: gossiping, wasting money, and begging.› [2]

Jundub Bin ʿAbdillāh and Ibn ʿAbbās (ﷺ) reported that Allāh's Messenger (ﷺ) said:

«من سمّعَ سمّعَ اللّهُ به، ومن راءى راءى اللّهُ به.»

‹Whoever does things for others to hear, Allāh will make the people hear about his sins (on the Day of Judgement). And whoever does things for others to see, Allāh will show his sins to others (on the Day of Judgement).› [3]

Once two men visited Salmān. Salmān brought before them bread and salt, which was all that he had at home, and said:

> "Had Allāh's Messenger (ﷺ) not prohibited us from being excessive in what we offer to our guests, we would have burdened ourselves for your sake." [4]

Avoiding Impermissible Utensils

One form of extravagance that some people practice in banquets and *walīmah*s is serving food in gold (rarely) or silver (often) plates or

---

1 *Al-Aʿrāf* 7:31.

2 Recorded by al-Bukhārī, Muslim, and others.

3 Recorded by al-Bukhārī, Muslim, and others.

4 Recorded by Aḥmad, al-Ḥākim, and others. Verified to be authentic by al-Albānī (*Irwā' ul-Ghalīl* no. 1957).

offering the attendees silverware that is made of gold or silver or is plated with one of these two metals. All of this is prohibited in *Islām*.

Huthayfah (⁜) reported that Allāh's Messenger (⁜) said:

«لا تلبسوا الحرير والديباج، ولا تشربوا في آنية الذهب والفضة،

فهي لهم في الدنيا، وهي لكم في الآخرة.»

‹Do not wear silk or *dībāj* (an expensive garment with silk lining and borders), nor sit on it; and do not eat or drink in silver or gold utensils; such things are for them (the disbelievers) in the worldly life and for us in the Hereafter.› [1]

Umm Salamah (⁜) reported that Allāh's Messenger (⁜) said:

«إن الذي يأكل أو يشرب في آنية الفضة والذهب، فإنما يجرجرُ

في بطنه ناراً من جهنم.»

‹Indeed, he who eats or drinks in gold or silver utensils only echoes in his stomach some of the Hell-fire.› [2]

Many scholars permit using silver-plated silverware — provided that the silver layer is so thin that it is negligible compared to the overall substance. However, even then, using that kind of silverware is a source of big *shubhah* (doubt), and is better to be totally avoided.

INVITING MANY PEOPLE

Within what is reasonable, one should try to bring to his food as many people as is possible. Jābir Bin 'Abdillāh (⁜) reported that Allāh's Messenger (⁜) said:

---

1   Recorded by al-Bukhārī, Muslim, and others.
2   Recorded by al-Bukhārī, Muslim, and others.

«أحب الطعام إلى اللّه ما كثُرت عليه الأيدي.»

‹The most beloved food to Allāh is that on which many hands gather.› [1]

Honoring The Guests

The guest has a right upon his host: he should be well treated and honored. Honoring the guest is a sign of true belief. Abū Hurayrah (ﷺ) reported that Allāh's Messenger (ﷺ) said:

«من كان يؤمن باللّه واليوم الآخر فليكرِمْ ضيفه، ومن كان يؤمن باللّه واليوم الآخر فليصِلْ رَحِمَهُ، ومن كان يؤمن باللّه واليوم الآخر فليقل خيراً أو ليصمت.»

‹He who believes in Allāh and the Last Day should honor his guest; he who believes in Allāh and the Last Day should be kind to his kin; and he who believes in Allāh and the Last Day should either say a good thing or remain silent.› [2]

Prophetic Manners in Honoring the Guests

One can learn a great deal about the fine manners of honoring the guests from a few *āyāt* describing Ibrāhīm's (ﷺ) treatment of his guests. Allāh (ﷻ) says:

﴿هَلْ أَتَىٰكَ حَدِيثُ ضَيْفِ إِبْرَٰهِيمَ ٱلْمُكْرَمِينَ ۝ إِذْ دَخَلُواْ عَلَيْهِ فَقَالُواْ سَلَٰمًا قَالَ سَلَٰمٌ قَوْمٌ مُّنكَرُونَ ۝ فَرَاغَ إِلَىٰٓ أَهْلِهِۦ فَجَآءَ بِعِجْلٍ سَمِينٍ ۝ فَقَرَّبَهُۥٓ إِلَيْهِمْ قَالَ أَلَا تَأْكُلُونَ ۝ فَأَوْجَسَ مِنْهُمْ خِيفَةً قَالُواْ

1 Recorded by Ibn Ḥibbān, al-Bayhaqī, and others. Verified to be authentic by al-Albānī (*Ṣaḥīḥ ul-Jāmiʿ* no. 171 & *aṣ-Ṣaḥīḥah* no. 895).

2 Recorded by al-Bukhārī, Muslim, and others.

لاَ تَخَفْ وَبَشَّرُوهُ بِغُلَٰمٍ عَلِيمٍ ۞﴾ الذاريات ٢٤-٢٨

«Has the story reached you of the honored guests of Ibrāhīm? That was when they entered his presence and said, "Peace [be upon you]!" He answered, "[And upon you be] peace, unfamiliar folks!" Then he turned quietly to his household, brought forth a fat [roasted] calf, and placed it before them. He said, "Will you not eat?" [When they did not reach for the meat] he conceived a fear of them; but they said, "Fear not," and gave him the glad tiding of [the birth of] a son who would be endowed with deep knowledge.» [1]

Ibn ul-Qayyim (ﷺ) provides a very inspiring coverage of the various lessons that one can learn from these *āyāt*. In what follows, we summarize his discussion in regard to honoring the guests [2].

1. Ibrāhīm went quietly and secretly (*rāgha*) to prepare the food. This indicates his hastening to honor and serve his guests in a secret manner in order not to embarrass them. This is to be contrasted with one who would purchase and prepare the food slowly and lazily, all in the presence of his guests. Such action would surely embarrass and disturb them.

2. For preparing the food, Ibrāhīm turned to no place other than his own household. This indicates that he had all what is usually needed to honor and serve the guests. He had no need of seeking anything from the neighbors or elsewhere.

3. Ibrāhīm brought the calf by himself. He served his guests personally rather than sending someone else to serve them.

4. Ibrāhīm brought before them a complete animal, and not just a

1 *Ath-Thāriyāt* 51:24-28.

2 The full text of Ibn ul-Qayyim is presented in the author's translation of *ar-Risālat ut-Tabūkiyyah*.

portion of it. This would allow them to select any part of it that they favor.

5. Ibrāhīm brought before them a fat animal, and not a skinny one. Furthermore, being a cow's young calf indicates that it was an expensive animal that should please the guests. His generosity and hospitality made him slaughter it despite its value.

6. Ibrāhīm brought the food and placed it in front of the guests rather than putting it in another room and having them move to reach it.

7. Rather than saying, "Go ahead - eat!", Ibrāhīm invited the guests to eat with very kind words, "Will you not eat?" — thereby giving them the choice to eat or not.

Manners for the Guests

There are also certain *ādāb* that should be exhibited by a guest who is invited to a *walīmah* or other meals. In what follows, we present some of the most important *ādāb*.

ANSWERING THE INVITATION IS A RELIGIOUS OBLIGATION

It is an obligation on every person who is invited to a *walīmah* to attend — unless he has a legitimate *Islāmic* excuse.

Ibn 'Umar (⌖) reported that Allāh's Messenger (⌖) said:

«إذا دعيَ أحدكم إلى الوليمة فليأتها، عرساً أو نحوه،

ومن لم يجب الدعوة فقد عصى اللّهَ ورسوله.»

‹When one of you is invited to a *walīmah*, he should attend it — if it is a wedding or something like it. And whoever does not answer the invitation, he has surely disobeyed Allāh and His Messenger.› [1]

1　Recorded by al-Bukhārī, Muslim, and others. The part specifying the wedding

Ibn Ḥajar concluded from this *ḥadīth* that answering the invitation is *wājib* because the one who does not do it is disobedient. [1]

Abū Mūsā al-Ash'arī (ﷺ) reported that Allāh's Messenger (ﷺ) said:

«فكوا العاني، وأجيبوا الداعي، وعودوا المريض.»

‹Set the (Muslim) captives free (by paying their ransom to the enemies), respond to the caller (to a *walīmah* and its likes), and visit the sick.› [2]

This carries a command from the Prophet (ﷺ), which again establishes that answering the invitation is a *wājib*.

With this understanding, one should answer the invitation with *īmān* (believing in its religious value) and *iḥtisāb* (seeking Allāh's reward for his attendance). If this is sincerely fulfilled, attending a *walīmah* becomes a rewardable act of worship (in the Hereafter) — besides being immediately rewardable in terms of the types of food served.

LEGITIMATE EXCUSES

A legitimate excuse that justifies not to attend a *walīmah* is any reason that would make attending it beyond a person's reasonable ability. Allāh (ﷻ) says:

﴿لاَ يُكَلِّفُ ٱللَّهُ نَفْساً إلاَّ وُسْعَهَا﴾ البقرة ٢٨٦

«Allāh does not burden a person beyond his capacity.» [3]

And He says:

---

is recorded by Abū Ya'la and verified to be authentic by al-Albānī (*Ādāb uz-Zifāf* p. 154).

1 *Fatḥ ul-Bārī*.

2 Recorded by al-Bukhārī.

3 *Al-Baqarah* 2:286.

$$\langle\text{يُرِيدُ ٱللَّهُ بِكُمُ ٱلْيُسْرَ وَلَا يُرِيدُ بِكُمُ ٱلْعُسْرَ}\rangle \text{ البقرة ١٨٥}$$

«Allāh intends for you ease and does not intend for you hardship.» [1]

And He says:

$$\langle\text{فَٱتَّقُوا۟ ٱللَّهَ مَا ٱسْتَطَعْتُمْ}\rangle \text{ التغابن ١٦}$$

«So have *taqwā* of Allāh as much as you are able.» [2]

Thus, the following could count as legitimate excuses:

1. Being invited to two *walīmah*s in two different places at the same time.

2. Having to undertake an expensive trip to attend the *walīmah*.

3. Having at the same time an important appointment that missing it would result in a serious harm in wealth, health, or well-being. Ex., a school examination, a business deal, etc.

However, even in such cases where one feels that he is justified in turning down an invitation to a *walīmah*, he should still contact the host and present his excuse ahead of time.

AVOIDING INVITATIONS THAT INVOLVE DISOBEDIENCE

One should refuse the invitation to a *walīmah* if he expects or discovers that it includes acts of disobedience to Allāh, such as drinking alcohol, music, dancing, mixing between men and women, and so on.

Ibn 'Umar (🙵) reported that Allāh's Messenger (ﷺ) said:

$$\text{«مَنْ كَانَ يُؤْمِنُ بِاللّٰهِ وَالْيَوْمِ الْآخِرِ فَلَا يَقْعُدْ عَلَى مَائِدَةٍ يُدَارُ عَلَيْهَا الْخَمْرُ.»}$$

---

1   *Al-Baqarah* 2:185.

2   *At-Taghābun* 64:16.

‹Whoever believes in Allāh and the Last Day may
not sit at a table on which *khamr* (any alcoholic
beverage) is circulated.› [1]

'Ali Bin Abī Ṭālib (⬥) reported that he prepared some food and
invited the Prophet (⬥). When the Prophet (⬥) arrived, he saw some
pictures [2] and turned to leave. 'Alī said, "O Allāh's Messenger, what
made you turn back — may my mother and father be your ransom?"
He (⬥) replied:

«إن في البيت سِتراً فيه تصاوير، وإن الملائكة لا تدخل بيتاً فيه تصاوير.»

‹Indeed, there is a curtain in the house on which
there are pictures; and the angels do not enter any
house in which there are pictures.› [3]

Aslam, the servant of 'Umar (⬥), reported that when 'Umar went
to ash-Shām (Palestine and the surrounding lands), one of the Christian
leaders prepared some food (in a church) and said to 'Umar, "Verily
I would like you and your companions to come and honor me."
'Umar (⬥) said:

"إنا لا ندخل كنائسَكم من أجل الصور التي فيها."

"Indeed, we do not enter your churches because of all
of the images that are in them." [4]

Abū Mas'ūd 'Uqbah Bin 'Amr (⬥) reported that a man once
prepared food for him and invited him. He asked the man, "Are there

---

1   Recorded by Aḥmad, at-Tirmithī, and others. Verified to be authentic by al-
     Albānī (*Irwā'ul-Ghalīl* no. 1949).

2   Those pictures contained prohibited images of animals, humans, or any being
     which has a soul.

3   Recorded by Ibn Mājah and Abū Ya'lā. Verified to be authentic by al-Albānī
     (*Ādāb uz-Zifāf* p. 161).

4   Recorded by al-Bayhaqī. Verified to be authentic by al-Albānī (*Ādāb uz-Zifāf*
     pp. 164-165).

pictures in the house?" The man replied, "Yes." Abū Mas'ūd then refused to enter until the image was smashed, then he entered. [1]

Al-Awzā'ī (رحمه الله) said:

"We do not attend a *walīmah* in which there are drums or lutes." [2]

EATING FROM THE FOOD

Even though it is obligatory to respond to the invitation, it is not obligatory to eat from the food. Depending on his situation, the guest may wish to eat or abstain from eating. In the second case, he should present his excuse for not eating in order to avoid offending the host.

Jābir Bin 'Abdillāh (رضي الله عنه) reported that Allāh's Messenger (ﷺ) said:

«إذا دعي أحدُكم إلى طعام فليجب، فإن شاء طعم،

وإن شاء ترك. »

‹When one of you is invited to food, he should respond to the invitation. If he then wishes, he may eat; and if he wishes, he may refrain from eating.› [3]

However, it is better to eat, even a little bit, as is mentioned in the next section.

WHAT SHOULD FASTING PEOPLE DO

A fasting person may remain fasting in a *walīmah*. Instead of eating, he should then supplicate for the host.

Abū Hurayrah and Ibn Mas'ūd (رضي الله عنهما) reported that Allāh's Messenger (ﷺ) said:

---

1   Recorded by al-Bayhaqī. Verified to be authentic by al-Albānī (*Ādāb uz-Zifāf* p. 165).

2   Recorded by Abū al-Ḥasan al-Ḥarbī (in *al-Fawā'id ul-Muntaqāt*). Verified to be authentic by al-Albānī (*Ādāb uz-Zifāf* p. 166).

3   Recorded by Muslim and others.

«إذا دعي أحدُكم إلى طعام فليجب، فإن كان مفطراً فليطعَم، وإن كان صائماً فليصل (فليدعُ بالبركة).»

‹When one of you is invited to food, he should answer the invitation. If he is not fasting, he should eat; and if he happens to be fasting, let him supplicate (asking blessings for the host).› [1]

Ibn ʿUmar (ﷺ) reported that Allāh's Messenger (ﷺ) said:

«أجيبوا هذه الدعوةَ إذا دُعيتم لها.»

‹Answer this invitation (to a *walīmah*) when you are invited.›

And Ibn ʿUmar used to attend when he was invited to a *walīmah* for wedding or otherwise, and would sometimes attend while fasting. [2]

However, if one is fasting a voluntary fasting, it is recommended for him to break his fast, especially if he expects his eating to bring joy to the host's heart.

Abū Saʿīd al-Khudrī (ﷺ) reported that he once prepared some food for Allāh's Messenger (ﷺ). The Messenger (ﷺ) came with some of his companions. When the food was brought, one man stayed away saying, "I am fasting." Allāh's Messenger (ﷺ) then said:

«دعاكم أخوكم وتكلف لكم! أفطر وصم مكانه يوماً إن شئت.»

‹Your brother has invited you and toiled for your sake! Break your fast and fast another day instead — if you wish.› [3]

---

1 Recorded by Muslim and others. The last part (about the blessings) is only reported by Ibn Masʿūd, recorded by aṭ-Ṭabarānī and Ibn us-Sunnī, and verified to be authentic by al-Albānī (*Irwā' ul-Ghalīl* no. 1953).

2 Recorded by al-Bukhārī, Muslim, and others.

3 Recorded by al-Bayhaqī, aṭ-Ṭabarānī (in *al-Awsaṭ*), and others. Verified to be authentic by al-Albānī (*Irwā' ul-Ghalīl* no. 1952 & *Ādāb uz-Zifāf* p. 159).

This *ḥadīth* also indicates that one is not obliged to make-up a voluntary fasting.

Seeking Permission to Enter

When one goes to a *walīmah* or its like, the host would usually be expecting him and there is not much necessity for seeking permission to enter — especially if it is held in a public place.

Abū Hurayrah (رضي الله عنه) reported that Allāh's Messenger (ﷺ) said:

«رسول الرجل إلى الرجلِ إذنُه.»

‹A messenger from one man to another (inviting him) gives him the permission (to attend).› [1]

In another report, Abū Hurayrah (رضي الله عنه) said that Allāh's Messenger (ﷺ) said:

«إذا دُعِيَ أحدُكم إلى طعامٍ فجاء مع الرسول، فذلك إذنٌ له.»

‹When one of you is invited to food and he comes with the messenger, that constitutes a permission for him.› [2]

Ibn Masʿūd (رضي الله عنه) said:

"إذا دُعيتَ فقد أُذن لك."

"When you are invited, you are (automatically) given the permission (to attend)." [3]

However, if the food is served in a private home, one must seek

---

1 Recorded by Abū Dāwūd, Ibn Ḥibbān, and al-Bukhārī in *al-Adab ul-Mufrad*. Verified to be authentic by al-Albānī (*Irwā'ul-Ghalīl* no. 1955).

2 Recorded by Abū Dāwūd and al-Bukhārī in *al-Adab ul-Mufrad*. Verified to be authentic by al-Albānī (*Irwā'ul-Ghalīl* no. 1955).

3 Recorded by al-Bukhārī in *al-Adab ul-Mufrad*. Verified to be authentic by al-Albānī (*Irwā'ul-Ghalīl* no. 1956).

permission to enter. Allāh (ﷻ) says:

﴿يَـٰٓأَيُّهَا ٱلَّذِينَ ءَامَنُواْ لَا تَدْخُلُواْ بُيُوتًا غَيْرَ بُيُوتِكُمْ حَتَّىٰ تَسْتَأْنِسُواْ وَتُسَلِّمُواْ عَلَىٰٓ أَهْلِهَا ۚ ذَٰلِكُمْ خَيْرٌ لَّكُمْ لَعَلَّكُمْ تَذَكَّرُونَ ۝﴾ النور ٢٧

«O you who believe! Do not enter houses other than your own until you have asked permission and greeted those in them; that is better for you — that you may remember.» [1]

Taking permission is important for a number of reasons, among which are the following:

1. The host should prepare himself for receiving the guests and make sure that their eyes would not fall on any of the women of the house improperly dressed.

   Sahl Bin Saʿd (رضي الله عنه) reported that Allāh's Messenger (ﷺ) said:

   «إنما جُعلَ الاستئذانُ من أجل البصر.»

   ‹Indeed, seeking permission to enter has only been ordained for the sake of the eye sight.› [2]

2. The host should be given the chance to ascertain that those who seek admission have all been invited. More about this will be discussed in the next sub-section.

Going Without Invitation

We saw from the above *ḥadīth*s in the previous sub-section that an invitation constitutes permission to attend. An uninvited person, therefore, has no guaranteed permission to be admitted — the host has the full right of either receiving him or asking him to leave.

---

1 *An-Nūr* 24:27.

2 Recorded by al-Bukhārī, Muslim, and others.

Abū Mas'ūd al-Anṣārī al-Badrī (ﷺ) reported that a man from *al-Anṣār* called Abū Shu'ayb had a slave who was a butcher. One day, while the Prophet (ﷺ) was sitting with (four of) his companions, Abū Shu'ayb visited him and noticed signs of hunger on his face. He rushed to his slave and ordered, "Prepare a meal sufficient for five persons so that I may invite the Prophet (ﷺ) with four other men." He then went and invited the Prophet (ﷺ) and the other four men. On their way to his house, a sixth man followed them. When they reached his door, the Prophet (ﷺ) said:

«إن هذا تبعَنا ، فإن شئتَ أن تأذن، وإن شئتَ رجع.»

‹Indeed, this man has followed us. If you wish you may admit him, and if you wish you may refuse him.›

Abū Shu'ayb (ﷺ) said, "No, I will admit him, O Allāh's Messenger."[1]

This *ḥadīth* indicates that the host may choose to accept or reject any uninvited guests, since he knows better how capable he is of entertaining his guests.

Unfortunately, we witness many cases where invited guests bring with them some uninvited individuals, thereby embarrassing the host and making it difficult for him to refuse them. They may even take personal offense if the host refused to admit their invitees. This is a clear violation of the *Sunnah* and deviation from proper guest-etiquettes.

GREETING WITH *SALĀM* AND SHAKING HANDS

When a Muslim meets his Muslim brothers, he should greet them with *salām*. Similarly, when one enters into someone's house for food or some other reason, he should greet the people who are present with *salām*. Allāh (ﷻ) says:

---

1 Recorded by al-Bukhārī, Muslim, and others.

﴿فَإِذَا دَخَلْتُم بُيُوتًا فَسَلِّمُوا عَلَىٰ أَنفُسِكُمْ تَحِيَّةً
مِّنْ عِندِ ٱللَّهِ مُبَٰرَكَةً طَيِّبَةً﴾ النور ٦١

«When you enter the houses, greet one another with a greeting from Allāh, blessed and good.» [1]

The host and other people who are present should respond with a greeting as good or better. Allāh (ﷻ) says:

﴿وَإِذَا حُيِّيتُم بِتَحِيَّةٍ فَحَيُّوا بِأَحْسَنَ مِنْهَآ أَوْ رُدُّوهَآ إِنَّ ٱللَّهَ
كَانَ عَلَىٰ كُلِّ شَيْءٍ حَسِيبًا ۝﴾ النساء ٨٦

«When you are greeted with a greeting, greet in return with what is better than it, or (at least) respond to it equally. Indeed, Allāh is ever a Careful Accountant over all things.» [2]

The reader is further referred to the two *ḥadīth*s of Ibn ʿUmar (p. 114) and Ṣuhayb (p. 115) that were cited early in this chapter.

Some people greet each other with non-*Islām*ic greetings, such as, "Good evening," "Hi," and so on. This should all be avoided, because Allāh has given us a better greeting: the *salām*. It carries a supplication of peace, and it is the greeting of the angels and the people of *Jannah*. [3]

Some people are also of the non-*Islām*ic habit of hugging and kissing each other whenever they meet. Hugging should only be reserved to meeting a person after a long absence, such as one who just came back from travel. In other situations, the Muslims should greet each other with *salām* and shake each others' hands.

Anas Bin Mālik (ﷺ) reported that a man asked the Prophet (ﷺ), "O Messenger of Allāh! When one of us meets his (Muslim) brother, should he bow his head to him?" He (ﷺ) replied, «لا.» **‹No!›** The man asked, "Should he embrace and kiss him?" He (ﷺ) replied, «لا.» **‹No!›**

1 *An-Nūr* 24:61.

2 *An-Nisā'* 4:86.

3 See, for example, *ar-Raʿd* 13:24.

The man then asked, "Should he shake his hand?" The Prophet (ﷺ) replied, «نعم.» ‹**Yes!**› [1]

There is indeed a great reward for shaking hands with a Muslim brother (or a woman with her Muslim sister). Al-Barā' Bin 'Āzib (ﷺ) reported that Allāh's Messenger (ﷺ) said:

«ما من مسلمين يلتقيان فيتصافحان إلا غُفر لهما قبل أن يتفرقا.»

‹Never would two Muslims meet and shake hands but they are forgiven even before they separate.› [2]

Abū Hurayrah (ﷺ) reported that Allāh's Messenger (ﷺ) said:

«إذا انتهى أحدُكم إلى المجلس فليسلّم، فإذا أراد أن يقومَ فليسلم، فليست الأولى بأحقَّ من الآخرة.»

‹When one of you reaches an assembly (of Muslims), let him give them *salām*. When he wishes to depart, let him give them *salām* as well. Indeed, the first (*salām*) is not more rightful than the last.› [3]

Uttering Allāh's Name over the Food

Before one starts eating, he should utter Allāh's name saying, "*Bismi 'llāh* — with Allāh's name (I eat)."

'Umar Bin Abī Salamah (ﷺ) reported that he was a young boy under custody of Allāh's Messenger (ﷺ), and that when he ate, his hand used to roam all over the plate. Allāh's Messenger (ﷺ) instructed him:

---

1 Recorded by at-Tirmithī. Verified to be *ḥasan* by al-Albānī (*Riyāḍ uṣ-Ṣāliḥīn* no. 893).

2 Recorded by Abū Dāwūd, at-Tirmithī, and others. Verified to be authentic by al-Albānī (*aṣ-Ṣaḥīḥah* no. 525).

3 Recorded by Abū Dāwūd, at-Tirmithī, and others. Verified to be authentic by al-Albānī (*aṣ-Ṣaḥīḥah* no. 183).

«يا غلام، سمِّ اللَّهَ، وكل بيمينِكَ، وكُل مما يليك.»

‹**Young boy! Utter Allāh's name, eat with your right hand, and eat from your side.**› [1]

Uttering Allāh's name brings blessings to the food. Waḥshiyy Bin Ḥarb (🙏) reported that a man said, "O Allāh's Messenger! We eat but do not feel satisfied." He asked, «فلعلكم تفترقون؟» ‹**Do you possibly eat separately?**› He said, "Yes." Allāh's Messenger (🙏) then said:

«اجتمعوا على طعامِكُم، واذكروا اسم اللَّه تعالى عليه، يُبَارك لكم فيه.»

‹**Gather upon your food; and utter Allāh's name – it would then be blessed for you.**› [2]

Uttering Allāh's name over the food prevents Satan from having any part in it. Jābir (🙏) reported that he heard Allāh's Messenger (🙏) say:

«إذا دخل الرجلُ بيتَه، فذكر اللَّهَ تعالى عند دخوله وعند طعامه، قال الشيطانُ لأصحابه: "لا مبيتَ لكم ولا عشاء." وإذا دخل فلم يذكر اللَّهَ تعالى عند دخوله، قال الشيطان: "أدركتم المبيت." وإذا لم يذكر اللَّهَ تعالى عند طعامه قال: "أدركتم المبيت والعشاء."»

‹**If a person utters Allāh's name when he enters his home and when he eats, Satan tells his companions, "Leave! There is no abode or food for you (in this house tonight)." But if he enters his house without mentioning Allāh's name, Satan says to his companions, "You have secured lodging." Then if he does not mention Allāh over his food Satan says,**

---

1   Recorded by al-Bukhārī, Muslim, and others.

2   Recorded by Aḥmad, Abū Dāwūd, and others. Verified to be *ḥasan* by al-Albānī (*Ṣaḥīḥ ul-Jāmiʿ* no. 142 & *aṣ-Ṣaḥīḥah* no. 664).

"You have secured both lodging and food."› [1]

If one forgets uttering Allāh's name before he starts eating and remembers later on during the meal, he may still utter it. ʿĀ'ishah (ﷺ) reported that Allāh's Messenger (ﷺ) said:

«إذا أكل أحدكم فليذكر اسمَ اللّه، فإن نسي أن يذكر اللّهَ في أوله فليقل: بسم اللّهِ أوله وآخرَه.»

‹When one of you eats, let him utter Allāh's name. If he forgets uttering Allāh's name in the beginning, let him say, "*Bismi 'llāhi awwalahū wa-'ākhirah* — with Allāh's name (I eat) from its beginning to its end."› [2]

Avoiding Criticizing the Food

All (*ḥalāl*) food is a favor from Allāh. One should not criticize it, because that could reflect dissatisfaction and ingratitude toward Allāh (ﷻ). Furthermore, that could offend and hurt the host.

Abū Hurayrah (ﷺ) reported:

"ما عاب رسول اللّه طعاماً قط. إن اشتهاه أكله، و إن كرهه تركه."

"Allāh's Messenger (ﷺ) never criticized any food. If he had desire for it he would eat it, and if he disliked it he would leave it." [3]

Moderateness in Eating

Whether one is at a *walīmah*, a restaurant, or eating at home, and whether the food is varied and delicious or plain and unappealing, one should never be excessive in eating. In addition to its harms to the

---

1 Recorded by Muslim.

2 Recorded by Abū Dāwūd, at-Tirmiṯhī, and others. Verified to be authentic by al-Albānī (*Irwā' ul-Ghalīl* no. 1965).

3 Recorded by al-Bukhārī, Muslim, and others.

health, overeating causes laziness and averts from remembering Allāh and being devoted in worship.

An important quality of a believer is that he does not overeat. Abū Hurayrah, Abū Mūsā al-Ash'arī, and 'Abdullāh Bin 'Umar (☺) reported that Allāh's Messenger (☺) said:

«إنّ المؤمن يأكل (ويشرب) في معيّ واحد ، والكافرُ يأكل

(ويشرب) في سبعة أمعاءٍ.»

‹Indeed, a believer eats in one intestine (i.e. is satisfied with little food), and a *kāfir* eats in seven intestines (eats too much).› [1]

The Prophet (☺) strongly prohibited gluttony and indicated that much of what the people eat is not necessary for them — rather, harmful! Al-Miqdām Bin Ma'd Yakrib (☺) reported that Allāh's Messenger (☺) said:

«ما ملأ آدميٌّ وعاءً شراً من بطنٍ. بحسب ابنِ آدمَ أُكلاتٌ

يُقِمْنَ صُلْبَه، فإن كان لا مَحالةَ، فثُلُثٌ لطعامه، وثلثٌ

لشرابه، وثلثٌ لنَفَسِهِ.»

‹A human being cannot fill a container worse than his stomach. Sufficient for a human being to eat a few mouthfuls to keep his back straight. But if that is not possible, he should reserve one third (of his stomach) for his food, one third for his drink, and one third for his breathing.› [2]

THE BLESSING OF EATING WITH OTHERS

We have seen earlier (Jābir's *hadīth* p. 117 & Wahshiyy's *hadīth*

---

1   Recorded by al-Bukhārī, Muslim, and others.

2   Recorded by at-Tirmithī, Aḥmad, and others. Verified to be authentic by al-Albānī (*aṣ-Ṣaḥīḥah* no. 2265).

p. 131) that eating with other people brings Allāh's blessings. To the same meaning, ʿUmar (ﷺ) reported that Allāh's Messenger (ﷺ) said:

«كُلوا جميعاً، ولا تفرّقوا، فإن البركةَ مع الجماعة.»

‹Eat together and not separately, for blessings come with company.› [1]

When eating in company, the food can suffice more people. Abū Hurayrah (ﷺ) reported that Allāh's Messenger (ﷺ) said:

«طعام الإثنين كافي الثلاثة، وطعام الثلاثة كافي الأربعة.»

‹The food of two persons is sufficient for three, and the food of three persons is sufficient for four.› [2]

Sitting Humbly and Eating from Around the Sides

Arrogance is a sign of ingratitude toward Allāh's favors. When eating, one is not supposed to recline or sit in a haughty manner; rather, one should sit humbly and eat with consideration.

ʿAbdullāh Bin Busr (ﷺ) reported that the Prophet (ﷺ) had a large platter called *al-Gharrāʾ* (the white one). It was so large that four men were needed to carry it. One day, a goat was given as gift to the Prophet (ﷺ) — and the food was then scarce. He told his family:

«اطبخوا هذه الشاة، وانظروا إلى هذا الدقيق فاخبزوه، اطبخوا وأثردوا عليه.»

‹Cook this goat, and take this flour and bake it. Cook and mix the bread with the meat.›

In the early morning, after the people had prayed the *ḍuḥā* voluntary prayers, *al-Gharrāʾ* was brought full of *tharīd* [3]. The people sat around it, and when they crowded, the Prophet (ﷺ) kneeled (with his knees

1 Recorded by Ibn Mājah. Verified to be *ḥasan* by al-Albānī (*Ṣaḥīḥ ul-Jāmiʿ* no. 4500 & *aṣ-Ṣaḥīḥah* no. 1686).

2 Recorded by al-Bukhārī and Muslim.

3 A dish made from bread and meat broth, with or without meat.

and toes touching the ground). A Bedouin said, "What kind of sitting is this?" The Prophet (ﷺ) replied:

«إن اللّهَ جعلني عبداً كريماً، ولم يجعلني جباراً عنيداً.»

‹Indeed, Allāh has made me an honored servant of His, and has not made me a stubborn tyrant.›

Then he (ﷺ) said:

«كُلوا من حواليْها ودَعوا ذِروتَها، يُبارَكْ فيها.»

‹Eat from around the sides (of the platter), and spare the raised (central) part — it will then be blessed for you.› [1]

In some of the reports of this *ḥadīth*, the Prophet (ﷺ) added:

«خذوا فكلوا؛ فوالذي نفس محمد بيده، لَيُفتَحَنَّ عليكم أرضُ فارسَ والرومِ، حتى يكثُر الطعام، فلا يذكرُ اسمُ اللّهِ عليه.»

‹Take and eat. By the One in Whose hand is Muḥammad's soul, the lands of the Persians and the Romans will be opened up for you, until the food will be so plentiful that Allāh's name will not be uttered over it.› [2]

This *ḥadīth* indicates that Allāh sends down blessings onto the center of a platter or tray from which a number of people are eating. If they eat from the sides and leave the center, the blessings will continue to flow from the center to all the sides.

To the same meaning, Ibn ʿAbbās (ﷺ) reported that Allāh's Messenger (ﷺ) said:

---

1 Recorded by Abū Dāwūd, Ibn Mājah, and others. Verified to be authentic by al-Albānī (*Irwā'ul-Ghalīl* no. 1966, 1981 and *aṣ-Ṣaḥīḥah* no. 393).

2 Recorded by Abū Bakr ash-Shāfiʿī (in *al-Fawā'id*), al-Bayhaqī, and others. Verified to be authentic by al-Albānī (*aṣ-Ṣaḥīḥah* no. 393).

«البركةُ تنزلُ وسَطَ الطعامِ، فكُلوا من حافَتَيْه، ولا تأكلوا من وسطه.»

‹Blessings descend upon the center of the food; so eat from the sides and do not eat from the center.› [1]

Avoiding Wasting Food

Nowadays, we see that many Muslims allow large quantities of food to go to waste, especially during *walīmah*s and other social functions — at the time when many other Muslims suffer from hunger and famines. This is contrary to the teachings of the *Sunnah*. The Prophet (ﷺ) was keen to retrieve even the small amount of food that stuck to his hand or plate.

Kaʿb Bin Mālik (رضي الله عنه) reported that Allāh's Messenger (ﷺ) used to eat with three fingers [2]. After finishing, he (ﷺ) would not clean his fingers until had licked them. [3]

Jābir (رضي الله عنه) reported that the Prophet (ﷺ) ordered his followers to lick their fingers and plates (after having eaten), and he (ﷺ) said:

«إنكم لا تدرون في أيِّ طعامِكم البركة.»

‹You do not know which part of your food has the blessings.› [4]

Even if some food falls from one's hand, he should not be reluctant to pick it up, clean it, and eat it! Jābir (رضي الله عنه) reported that Allāh's Messenger (ﷺ) said:

«إن الشيطانَ يحضرُ أحدكم عند كل شيءٍ من شأنه، حتى يحضرَه

1 Recorded by Abū Dāwūd, at-Tirmithī, and others. Verified to be authentic by al-Albānī (*Irwā' ul-Ghalīl* no. 1980/1).

2 Note that there is nothing wrong in eating with silverware. However, it would be more rewarding to follow the Prophet's (ﷺ) way of eating with their three fingers. This applies particularly to food items that come in big chunks like bread or dates.

3 Recorded by Muslim, Abū Dāwūd, and others.

4 Recorded by Muslim and others.

عند طعامه. فإذا وقعت لقمة أحدِكم فليأخذها، فليُمِطْ ما كان بها من أذىً، وليأكُلْها ولا يدعُها للشيطان. ولا يمسح يده بالمِنديل، حتى يلعقَ أصابعه، فإنه لا يدري في أي طعامه البركةُ.»

‹Indeed, Satan comes to each of you during all of his affairs, including his eating. If one of you drops a bite of food, let him pick it up, remove any dirt from it, and eat it and not leave it for Satan. Furthermore, one should not wipe his hand with a handkerchief (from the remnants of food) — until he had licked his fingers, for he cannot know in which part of the food is the blessing.› [1]

PRAISING ALLĀH AND SUPPLICATING TO HIM AFTER EATING

After eating, one should express his gratitude to the One Who granted him the food by praising Him. Anas (ﷺ) reported that Allāh's Messenger (ﷺ) said:

«إن اللّهَ ليرضى عن العبد أن يأكلَ الأكلةَ فيحمَدُه عليها، أو يشربَ الشَّربةَ فيحمدُه عليها.»

‹Indeed, Allāh is pleased with a servant (of His) who eats some food and praises Him for it, or drinks a drink and praises Him for it.› [2]

Ibn ʿAbbās (ﷺ) reported that Allāh's Messenger (ﷺ) said:

«من أطعمه اللّهُ طعاماً فليقل: "اللّهم بارك لنا فيه، وأطعمنا خيراً منه." ومن سقاه اللّهُ لبناً فليقل: "اللّهم بارك لنا فيه، وزدنا منه." فإنه ليس شيءٌ يُجزئُ من الطعام والشراب غيرُ اللبن.»

---

1 Recorded by Muslim.

2 Recorded by Muslim and others.

‹He whom Allāh feeds food should say, "*Allāhumma bārik lanā fīhi wa-rzuqnā khayran minh* — O Allāh, bless it for us and provide us with a better food." And he whom Allāh gives milk to drink should say, "*Allāhumma bārik lanā fīhi wa-zidnā minh* — O Allāh, bless it for us and give us more of it," because no food or drink is sufficient (in nutrition) except milk.› [1]

Abū Umāmah (🕮) reported that when the Prophet (🕮) finished eating he would say:

«الحمد لله حمداً كثيراً طيباً مباركاً فيه، غير مُكافَئٍ،

ولا مُودَّعٍ، ولا مُستغنىً عنهُ ربَّنا.»

‹*Al-ḥamdu lillāhi, ḥamdan kathīran ṭayyiban mubārakan fīhi, ghayra mukāfa'in, wa-lā muwadda'in, wa-lā mustaghnan 'anhu rabbanā* — All praise is due to Allāh — a praise that is plentiful, pure, and full of blessings. (Your sustenance) cannot be equally repaid, we consistently need it, and we cannot live without it, O our Lord!› [2]

Mu'ā<u>th</u> Bin Anas al-Juhanī (🕮) reported that Allāh's Messenger (🕮) said:

«من أكل طعاماً، ثم قال: "الحمد لله الذي أطعمني هذا الطعامَ

ورزَقَنيه من غير حول مني ولا قوة، " غُفر له ما تقدم من ذنبه.»

‹Whoever eats some food and then says, "*Al-ḥamdu li-'llāh il-la<u>th</u>ī aṭ'amanī hā<u>th</u>ā wa-razaqanīhi min ghayri ḥawlin minnī wa-lā quwwah* — All praise is due to Allāh who fed me this and provided it for me

---

1   Recorded by Aḥmad, Abū Dāwūd, and others. Verified to be *ḥasan* by al-Albānī (*Ṣaḥīḥ ul-Jāmi'* no. 6045 & *aṣ-Ṣaḥīḥah* no. 2320).

2   Recorded by al-Bukhārī and others.

without any might or power from myself," all his past sins will be forgiven.› [1]

A man who served the Prophet (ﷺ) for eight years said that when he brought the food before him he would say, «بسم الله.» ‹***Bismillāh* — with Allāh's name.›** When he finished eating, he would say:

«اللّهم أطعمت وأسقيت، وأغنيت وأقنيت، وهديتَ وأحييت،
فلك الحمد على ما أعطيت.»

***‹Allāhumma aṭʿamta wa-asqayta, wa-aghnayta wa-aqnayta, wa-hadayta wa-aḥyayta, falaka 'l-ḥamdu ʿalā mā aʿṭayta* — O Allāh, You have fed (me), given (me) drink, sufficed (me) from needing others, endowed (me) with everything, guided (me), and given (me) life; so to You is all praise for all that You have granted.›** [2]

Supplicating for the Hosts

In addition to praising Allāh, one should show gratitude to the people who fed him. This is best done by supplicating for them.

Al-Miqdād Bin al-Aswad (ﷺ) reported that Allāh's Messenger (ﷺ) supplicated for those who fed him or gave him something to drink, saying:

«اللّهم أطعِم من أطعمني واْسقِ من سقاني.»

***‹Allāhumma aṭʿim man aṭʿamanī, wa-sqi man saqānī* — O Allāh, feed the one who fed me, and give drink to the one who gave me drink.›** [3]

---

1 Recorded by Ibn Mājah, Abū Dāwūd, and others. Verified to be *ḥasan* by al-Albānī (*Ṣaḥīḥ ul-Jāmiʿ* no. 6086 & *Irwā' ul-Ghalīl* no. 1989).

2 Recorded by Aḥmad, an-Nasā'ī (in *al-Kubrā*), and others. Verified to be authentic by al-Albānī (*aṣ-Ṣaḥīḥah* no. 71 & *al-Kalim uṭ-Ṭayyib*).

3 Recorded by Muslim and others.

ʿAbdullāh Bin Busr (ﷺ) reported that Allāh's Messenger (ﷺ) once stayed as a guest with his father. They put before him some food and he ate. Then they brought some drink, and he drank from it then handed it to the person sitting to his right. As the Prophet (ﷺ) mounted his animal to leave, ʿAbdullāh's father asked him to supplicate for them, and he (ﷺ) said:

«اللّهم بارك لهم فيما رزقتهم، واْغفر لهم، واْرحمهم.»

‹*Allāhumma bārik lahum fīmā razaqtahum, wa-ghfir lahum, wa-rḥamhum* — O Allāh! Bless for them that which You provided them, forgive them, and have mercy upon them.› [1]

Anas (ﷺ) reported that the Prophet (ﷺ) once visited Saʿd Bin ʿUbādah (ﷺ). Saʿd offered him some raisins, and the Prophet (ﷺ) ate and then said:

«أفطر عندكم الصائمون، وأكل طعامكم الأبرارُ،
وصلّت عليكم الملائكةُ.»

‹*Afṭara ʿindakum uṣ-ṣāʾimūn, wa-akala ṭaʿāmakum ul-abrār, wa-ṣallat ʿalaykum ul-malāʾikah* — May the fasting people break their fast at your place; and may the righteous eat from your food; and may the angels supplicate for you.› [2]

Departure

If one is invited for a meal, he should not inconvenience the host and his household by coming too early and waiting for the food to be ready. Allāh (ﷻ) instructed the believers about this etiquette in regard to the Prophet (ﷺ):

---

1 Recorded by Muslim.

2 Recorded by Abū Dāwūd, Ibn Mājah, and others. Verified to be authentic by al-Albānī (*Ṣaḥīḥ ul-Jāmiʿ* no. 1137 (from the report of Ibn uz-Zubayr) & *Ādāb uz-Zifāf* p. 170).

﴿يَـٰٓأَيُّهَا ٱلَّذِينَ ءَامَنُواْ لَا تَدْخُلُواْ بُيُوتَ ٱلنَّبِيِّ، إِلَّآ أَن يُؤْذَنَ لَكُمْ
إِلَىٰ طَعَامٍ، غَيْرَ نَـٰظِرِينَ إِنَـٰهُ.﴾ الأحزاب ٥٣

«O you who believe! Do not enter the houses of the Prophet except when you are invited for a meal — without awaiting its readiness.» [1]

Also, one should not inconvenience the host by staying too long after finishing eating. Allāh (ﷻ) says:

﴿وَلَـٰكِنْ إِذَا دُعِيتُمْ فَٱدْخُلُواْ، فَإِذَا طَعِمْتُمْ فَٱنتَشِرُواْ، وَلَا
مُسْتَـْٔنِسِينَ لِحَدِيثٍ؛ إِنَّ ذَٰلِكُمْ كَانَ يُؤْذِي ٱلنَّبِيَّ فَيَسْتَحْيِي
مِنكُمْ؛ وَٱللَّهُ لَا يَسْتَحْيِي مِنَ ٱلْحَقِّ.﴾ الأحزاب ٥٣

«But when you are invited, enter; and when you have eaten, disperse without seeking to remain for conversation. Indeed, that was troubling the Prophet, and he is shy of (dismissing) you. But Allāh is not shy of the truth.» [2]

At departure, one should give *salām* as he did when he entered. In this regard, we again cite Abū Hurayrah's (رضي الله عنه) *ḥadīth* that Allāh's Messenger (ﷺ) said:

«إذا انتهى أحدُكم إلى المجلس فليسلِّم، فإذا أراد أن يقومَ
فليسلم، فليست الأولى بأحقَّ من الآخرة.»

‹When one of you reaches an assembly (of Muslims), let him give them *salām*. When he wishes to depart, let him give them *salām* as well. Indeed, the first (*salām*) is not more rightful than the last.› [3]

---

1 *Al-Aḥzāb* 33:53.

2 *Al-Aḥzāb* 33:53.

3 Recorded by Abū Dāwūd, at-Tirmithī, and others. Verified to be authentic by

al-Albānī (*aṣ-Ṣaḥīḥah* no. 183).

CHAPTER 8

FORBIDDEN MARRIAGES

Permanently Prohibited Women

INTRODUCTION

Permanently prohibited women are the women that a man may never marry. Permanent prohibition can be a result of blood, marriage, or foster (breast-feeding) relationships. A man is a *maḥram* to any woman who is permanently prohibited to him.

Allāh (ﷻ) mentions the permanently prohibited women in the following *āyāt*:

﴿وَلَا تَنكِحُوا۟ مَا نَكَحَ ءَابَآؤُكُم مِّنَ ٱلنِّسَآءِ إِلَّا مَا قَدْ سَلَفَ ۚ إِنَّهُۥ كَانَ فَـٰحِشَةً وَمَقْتًا وَسَآءَ سَبِيلًا ۝﴾ النساء ٢٢

«And do not marry the women whom your fathers had married — except what has already passed. Indeed, that was a shameful and hateful act (to Allāh), and an evil way.» [1]

﴿حُرِّمَتْ عَلَيْكُمْ أُمَّهَـٰتُكُمْ وَبَنَاتُكُمْ وَأَخَوَٰتُكُمْ وَعَمَّـٰتُكُمْ وَخَـٰلَـٰتُكُمْ وَبَنَاتُ ٱلْأَخِ وَبَنَاتُ ٱلْأُخْتِ وَأُمَّهَـٰتُكُمُ ٱلَّـٰتِىٓ أَرْضَعْنَكُمْ وَأَخَوَٰتُكُم مِّنَ ٱلرَّضَـٰعَةِ وَأُمَّهَـٰتُ نِسَآئِكُمْ وَرَبَـٰٓئِبُكُمُ ٱلَّـٰتِى فِى حُجُورِكُم مِّن نِّسَآئِكُمُ ٱلَّـٰتِى دَخَلْتُم بِهِنَّ فَإِن لَّمْ تَكُونُوا۟ دَخَلْتُم بِهِنَّ فَلَا جُنَاحَ عَلَيْكُمْ وَحَلَـٰٓئِلُ أَبْنَآئِكُمُ ٱلَّذِينَ مِنْ أَصْلَـٰبِكُمْ وَأَن

---

1 *An-Nisā'* 4:22.

تَجْمَعُواْ بَيْنَ ٱلْأُخْتَيْنِ إِلاَّ مَا قَدْ سَلَفَ، إِنَّ ٱللَّهَ كَانَ غَفُورًا رَّحِيمًا ۝﴾ النساء ٢٣

«Prohibited to you (for marriage) are your mothers, daughters, sisters, paternal aunts, maternal aunts, brother's daughters, sister's daughters, foster mothers who breast-fed you, foster sisters, wives' mothers, step-daughters under your custody and born of your wives with whom you have had intercourse — but if you have not had intercourse with them, there is no sin upon you (if you marry them) —, the wives of your sons who are your own offspring, and that you simultaneously marry two sisters — except for what has already passed. Indeed, Allāh is Forgiving and Merciful.» [1]

﴿وَٱلْمُحْصَنَـٰتُ مِنَ ٱلنِّسَآءِ، إِلاَّ مَا مَلَكَتْ أَيْمَـٰنُكُمْ، كِتَـٰبَ ٱللَّهِ عَلَيْكُمْ، وَأُحِلَّ لَكُم مَّا وَرَآءَ ذَالِكُمْ أَن تَبْتَغُواْ بِأَمْوَالِكُم، مُّحْصِنِينَ غَيْرَ مُسَـٰفِحِينَ، فَمَا ٱسْتَمْتَعْتُم بِهِ مِنْهُنَّ فَئَاتُوهُنَّ أُجُورَهُنَّ فَرِيضَةً، وَلاَ جُنَاحَ عَلَيْكُمْ فِيمَا تَرَاضَيْتُم بِهِ مِن بَعْدِ ٱلْفَرِيضَةِ، إِنَّ ٱللَّهَ كَانَ عَلِيمًا حَكِيمًا ۝﴾ النساء ٢٤

«And (also prohibited to you are) all married women, except those (captives and slaves) that your right hands possess. This is Allāh's decree upon you. And are lawful to you all (women) beyond these, provided that you seek them (in marriage) with gifts from your monies, desiring chastity, not unlawful sexual intercourse. So for those whom you enjoy (in marriage) from among them, give them their due compensation (*mahr*) as an obligation. And there is no blame upon you for what you mutually agree (to

---

1 *An-Nisā* 4:23.

give) beyond the obligation. Indeed, Allāh is Knowing and Wise.» [1]

PROHIBITION BASED ON BLOOD RELATIONSHIPS

From the above, we conclude that the women who are permanently prohibited for a man because of blood relationships are seven types:

1. His mothers (including his grandmothers from both sides, and further up).

2. His daughters and granddaughters (and further down).

3. His sisters (both full and half-sisters).

4. His paternal aunts (including his father's, grandfathers', mother's, and grandmothers' paternal aunts, and further up).

5. His maternal aunts (including his father's, grandfathers', mother's, and grandmothers' maternal aunts, and further up).

6. His brothers' (both full and half-brothers) daughters and granddaughters (and further down).

7. His sisters' (both full and half-sisters) daughters and granddaughters (and further down).

PROHIBITION BASED ON MARITAL RELATIONSHIPS

The women who are permanently prohibited for a man because of marital relationships are four types:

1. The wives of his fathers (and grandfathers, and further up). This prohibition occurs as soon as a father executes his marriage contract on a woman, even if he does not perform intercourse with her.

---

1 *An-Nisā̄* 4:24.

2. The wives of his sons (and grandsons, and further down). This prohibition occurs as soon as a son executes his marriage contract on a woman, even if he does not perform intercourse with her.

3. His wive's mothers (and grandmothers, and further up). This prohibition occurs as soon as a man executes his marriage contract on a woman, even if he does not perform intercourse with her.

4. The daughters (and granddaughters, and further down) of the wives with whom he performed intercourse.

In regard to step-daughters (Case 4 above), most scholars hold the opinion that they are all prohibited, without exception — as soon as their step-father performs intercourse with their mother. They say that the "custody" restriction in the above *āyah* (4:23) is a description applicable to all step-daughters.

However, a very viable opinion is that the "custody" is intended as a restriction, and that a step-daughter who did not live in her step-father's house is only temporarily prohibited to him — as long as he is married to her mother. This opinion was held by ʿAlī (ﷺ).

Mālik Bin Aws Bin al-Ḥadathān reported that he had a wife who bore him some children and then died. He was extremely sorrowful for her death. He met ʿAlī (ﷺ) who asked him, "What is wrong with you?" He replied, "The wife has died." He asked him, "Did she have a daughter?" He said, "Yes, and she is at aṭ-Ṭā'if (a town to the south of Makkah)." He asked, "Was she ever under your custody?" He said, "No." He suggested, "Marry her then." He said, "But what about Allāh's prohibition of 'Your step-daughters who are under your custody'?" He said, "Indeed, she was not under your custody. Indeed, that only applies if she lived in your house." [1]

Prohibition Based on Milk Relationships

Breast-feeding a baby gives him (or her) nutrition and growth through the milk of the breast-feeding mother. When a woman breast-feeds a

1 Recorded by ʿAbd ur-Razzāq and Ibn Abī Ḥātim. Verified to be authentic by al-Albānī (*Irwā'ul-Ghalīl* no. 1880).

baby-boy, he becomes related to her in a way similar to her delivered sons.

'Ā'ishah, Ibn 'Abbās, and 'Alī (ﷺ) reported that Allāh's Messenger (ﷺ) said:

«إن اللّهَ حرّم من الرضاعِ ما حرّمَ من الولادةِ (النسبِ).»

‹Indeed, Allāh has prohibited (of marriages), based on breast-feeding, what He has prohibited based on birth (or blood-relationships).› [1]

However, for breast-feeding to result in prohibitive relationships, it must satisfy the following conditions:

1. It should be performed on five or more distinct suckles.

2. The baby should be hungry and should drink its fill in each suckle.

3. All prohibiting suckles should take place before the baby's weaning age of two.

'Ā'ishah (ﷺ) reported that Allāh's Messenger (ﷺ) said:

«لا تُحَرِّمُ المصّةُ ولا المصّتان.»

‹One or two suckles do not cause prohibition.› [2]

Umm ul-Faḍl (ﷺ) reported that when Allāh's Prophet (ﷺ) was in her house once, a bedouin came and asked him, "O Prophet of Allāh! I have just married a second wife, but my first wife claims that she suckled her on one or two occasions." Allāh's Messenger (ﷺ) said:

«لا تُحَرِّمُ الإملاجةُ ولا الإملاجتان.»

---

1 Recorded by al-Bukhārī, Muslim, and others. Review *Irwā'ul-Ghalīl* no. 1876 for the various narrations of this *ḥadīth*.

2 Recorded by Muslim, Abū Dāwūd, and others.

‹One or two suckles do not cause prohibition.› [1]

ʿĀʾishah (ﷺ) reported that Allāh's Messenger (ﷺ) said:

«أنظرن من إخوانُكنَّ، فإنما الرَّضاعةُ من المجاعة.»

‹Check (O Women) who are your true brothers, because breast-feeding (that causes brotherhood) is that which satisfies the hunger.› [2]

Umm Salamah and ʿAbdullāh Bin az-Zubayr (ﷺ) reported that Allāh's Messenger (ﷺ) said:

«لا يُحَرِّمُ من الرَّضاعِ إلا مافتق الأمعاء وكان قبل الفطام.»

‹Breast-feeding does not cause prohibition unless it expands the intestines (i.e., satisfies the baby's hunger), and takes place before weaning.› [3]

ʿĀʾishah (ﷺ) reported:

> "It was first revealed in the *Qurʾān* that, **'Ten known suckles cause prohibition.'** Five of those were then dropped, and it became, **'Five known suckles cause prohibition.'** This was the final state when Allāh's Messenger (ﷺ) passed away." [4]

In the following, we mean by "foster mother" the woman who breast-fed a person according to the above-listed conditions. And a "foster father" is the man who was married to the foster mother at the time of breast-feeding that person; he is thus the person who caused the foster mother's milk.

---

1 Recorded by Muslim, Ibn Mājah, and others.

2 Recorded by al-Bukhārī, Muslim, and others.

3 Recorded by at-Tirmithī and Ibn Mājah. Verified to be authentic by al-Albānī (*Irwāʾ ul-Ghalīl* no. 2150 & *Ṣaḥīḥ ul-Jāmiʿ* no. 7495, 7633).

4 Recorded by Mālik, Muslim, and others.

The women who are permanently prohibited for a man because of breast-feeding relationships are seven types:

1. His foster mother.

2. His foster mother's mother — she counts as his (maternal) grandmother.

3. His foster father's mother — she counts as his (paternal) grandmother.

4. The sisters of his foster mother — they count as his maternal aunts.

5. The sisters of his foster father — they count as his paternal aunts.

6. His foster mother's granddaughters — they count as his nieces.

7. His foster sisters, and they are of three types:

   a) The foster sisters breast-fed by the same foster mother, and from the same husband's milk — whether at the same time or at different times. They count as his full sisters.

   b) The foster sisters breast-fed by the same foster mother, and from two different husbands' milks. They count as his half maternal-sisters.

   c) The foster sisters breast-fed by a wife of his foster father other than his foster mother — whether the breast-feeding took place at the same time or at different times. Those count as his half-paternal sisters.

It is important to note here that the foster relationships only apply to the breast-fed person and his offspring. They do not apply to other relatives, such as his blood brothers and sisters.

For example, let us assume that a person "A" has a foster sister "B", a blood brother "C", and a son "D". In this case, "A" and "D" are prohibited from marrying "B", but "C" is not.

Temporarily Prohibited Women or Marriages

Temporary prohibition is that which prevents a man from marrying a woman under certain conditions. If the conditions cease to hold, the prohibition ends and the woman becomes permissible for him.

The temporarily prohibited women are the following:

Marrying More than Four Women

If a man has four wives, all other women become temporarily prohibited for him. This means that he may not consider any additional woman for marriage unless he divorces one of his wives.

It is not allowed for a man to have more than four wives in *Islām*. Even for those who had more than four wives before embracing *Islām*, the Prophet (ﷺ) commanded them to select four of them and divorce the rest. Ibn ʿUmar (ﷺ) reported that Ghaylān Bin Salamah had ten wives when he embraced *Islām*. Allāh's Messenger (ﷺ) told him:

«أمسك منهن أربعاً، وفارق سائرهن.»

‹Keep four of them and divorce the rest.› [1]

Simultaneously Marrying Two Sisters

As long as a man is married to a particular woman, all of her sisters become temporarily prohibited for him; he may not marry any of them unless he divorces their sister.

Abū Hurayrah (ﷺ) reported that Allāh's Messenger (ﷺ) said:

«لا تُنكحُ المرأةُ على عمتها، ولا العمةُ على ابنة أخيها، ولا
المرأةُ على خالتها، ولا الخالة على بنت أختها، ولا الكبرى
على الصغرى، ولا الصغرى على الكبرى.»

---

1 Recorded by at-Tirmiḏhī, Ibn Mājah, and others. Verified to be authentic by al-Albānī (*Irwā' ul-Ghalīl* no. 1883).

‹A woman may not be simultaneously married with her paternal aunt (to the same man), nor a paternal aunt with her niece, nor a niece with her maternal aunt, nor a maternal aunt with her niece, nor an older sister with her younger sister, nor a younger sister with her older sister.› [1]

SIMULTANEOUSLY MARRYING AUNTS AND THEIR NIECES

We see from Abū Hurayrah's above *hadīth* that it is not permissible to simultaneously marry an aunt and her niece. A man would have to divorce one of the two before he may marry the other.

To the same meaning, Abū Hurayrah, Jābir, Ibn 'Abbās, Abū Sa'īd, Ibn 'Umar, and 'Alī (⬥) all reported [2] that Allāh's Messenger (⬥) said:

«لا يُجمعُ بين المرأة وعمتها، ولا بين المرأة وخالتها.»

‹One may not simultaneously have (as wives) a woman and her paternal aunt, nor a woman and her maternal aunt.› [3]

WOMEN MARRIED TO OTHER MEN

This is clearly expressed in the above *āyah* of *Sūrat un-Nisā* (4:24).

The same applies to a woman who has been divorced a non-terminal divorce (first two times) and is still in her *'iddah*. Such a woman is considered to be still under her husband's charge and no one may approach her for marriage before the completion of her *'iddah*.

---

1 Recorded by Abū Dāwūd, an-Nasā'ī, and others. Verified to be authentic by al-Albānī (*Irwā'ul-Ghalīl* no. 1882).

2 The various narrations of this *hadīth* are collected by al-Albānī in *Irwā'ul-Ghalīl* no. 1882.

3 Recorded by al-Bukhārī, Muslim, and others.

ADULTERESSES

It is prohibited to marry a woman who is known to be an adulteress or a prostitute — unless she demonstratedly repents. Allāh (ﷻ) says:

﴿ٱلزَّانِي لَا يَنكِحُ إِلَّا زَانِيَةً أَوْ مُشْرِكَةً، وَٱلزَّانِيَةُ لَا يَنكِحُهَا إِلَّا زَانٍ أَوْ مُشْرِكٌ، وَحُرِّمَ ذَٰلِكَ عَلَى ٱلْمُؤْمِنِينَ ۝﴾ النور ٣

«A fornicator does not marry but a female fornicator or polytheist; and none marries a female fornicator but a fornicator or a polytheist. Such a thing is forbidden to the believers.» [1]

Ḥabīb al-Muʿallim reported that a man from al-Kūfah (in Iraq) came to ʿAmr Bin Shuʿayb [2] and said, "Would it not surprise you to learn that al-Ḥasan (al-Baṣrī) says that a whipped fornicator may not marry but a female whipped fornicator like himself?" ʿAmr replied, "What is it that surprises you? This has been reported to us from Saʿīd al-Maqbirī from Abū Hurayrah (ﷺ) that Allāh's Messenger (ﷺ) said:

«لا ينكح الزاني المجلودُ إلاّ مثله.»

‹A whipped fornicator may not marry but one who is like himself›" [3]

In regard to this *ḥadīth*, ash-Shawkānī (ﷺ) said:

"This is a general description applicable to anyone who is known to commit *zinā*. It presents evidence that it is not permissible for a woman to marry a man who is known to commit *zinā*. Similarly, it is not permissible for a man to marry a woman who is known to commit

1 *An-Nūr* 24:3.

2 ʿAmr Bin Shuʿayb is the son of Shuʿayb Bin Muḥammad Bin ʿAbdillāh Bin ʿAmr Bin al-ʿĀṣ. He is thus the great-grandson of ʿAbdullāh Bin ʿAmr (ﷺ).

3 Recorded by Abū Dāwūd, Aḥmad, and al-Ḥākim. Verified to be authentic by al-Albānī (*aṣ-Ṣaḥīḥah* no. 2444).

> *zinā*. This is further indicated by the *āyah* (*an-Nūr* 24:3)." [1]

ʿAmr Bin Shuʿayb also reported from his father from his grandfather that Marthid Bin Abī Marthid al-Ghanawī used to help the Muslim captives run away from Makkah. A prostitute in Makkah called ʿAnāq was his girlfriend. He came to Allāh's Messenger (ﷺ) and asked him, "O Allāh's Messenger (ﷺ), may I marry ʿAnāq?" Allāh's Messenger (ﷺ) did not say anything until the above *āyah* was revealed, so he summoned him and said, «لا تنكحها.» **‹Do not marry her.›** [2]

Ibn ul-Qayyim (رحمه الله) said:

> "What explains the prohibition is that this crime causes harm to the husband's mattress (i.e., honor), and spoils the kinship relationships that Allāh established among the people so that they would pursue their affairs … Thus, one of the beauties of the *sharīʿah* is its prohibition of marrying an adulteress — until she repents and purifies her womb." [3]

Ibn ul-Qayyim (رحمه الله) also said:

> "As for marrying an adulteress, Allāh has indicated its prohibition in *Sūrat un-Nūr*, and He indicated that anyone who marries her is a fornicator or a *mishrik*. That is because he either believes in Allāh's commands and the obligation of following them, or does not believe. In the latter case, he would be a *mishrik*, and in the first he would be a fornicator because he knew Allāh's ruling and disobeyed it." [4]

---

1 *Nayl ul-Awṭār* 6:283.

2 Recorded by Abū Dāwūd, an-Nasāʾī, and others. Verified to be authentic by al-Albānī (*Irwāʾ ul-Ghalīl* no. 1886).

3 *Ighāthat ul-Lahfān* 1:66.

4 *Zād ul-Maʿād* 5:114.

MUSHRIK WOMEN

A *mushrik* woman may not be married unless she embraces *Islām*. The subject of marrying non-Muslim women is covered in detail in a subsequent section.

MARRIAGE DURING *IHRĀM*

A person who goes for *Hajj* or *'Umrah* is prohibited from courting or marriage while he is in the state of *ihrām* [1].

'Uthmān (⟨⟩) reported that Allāh's Messenger (⟨⟩) said:

«لا يَنكِحُ المُحرِمُ، ولا يُنكَح، ولا يَخطِب.»

‹**A person in a state of *ihrām* may not marry, be married, or propose to someone (for marriage).**› [2]

MARRYING A PREGNANT CAPTIVE-WOMAN

Allāh's Messenger (⟨⟩) prohibited having intercourse with female war-captives (whether as concubines or regular wives) until they purify their wombs from previous relationships.

Abū Saʿīd al-Khudrī (⟨⟩) reported that Allāh's Messenger (⟨⟩) said in regard to the war-captives of Awṭās battle:

«لا توطأ حامِلٌ حتى تضع، ولا غير ذات حمل حتى تحيض.»

‹**One may not copulate with a pregnant woman until she delivers, nor with a non-pregnant woman until she menstruates (one time).**› [3]

Ruwayfiʿ Bin Thābit (⟨⟩) reported that Allāh's Messenger (⟨⟩)

---

1   *Ihrām:* A sacred temporary state for a pilgrim during which he renounces many of the worldly pleasures such as women and perfume.

2   Recorded by Muslim and others.

3   Recorded by Abū Dāwūd, al-Bayhaqī, and others. Verified to be authentic by al-Albānī (*Sahīh ul-Jāmiʿ* no. 7479 & *Irwāʾ ul-Ghalīl* no. 187).

said:

«من كان يؤمن بالله واليوم الآخِر فلا يسق ماءَه زرعَ غيره، ومن كان يؤمن بالله واليوم الآخِر فلا يأتِ سبياً من السبي حتى يستبرئها.»

> **‹Whoever believes in Allāh and the Last Day should not irrigate someone else's plantation with his water (i.e., sperm), and whoever believes in Allāh and the Last Day should not copulate with a captive of war until she purifies her womb (by menses).›** [1]

Ibn ʿUmar (ﷺ) said:

> "When a slave-girl who has had intercourse with men is given away or sold or freed, she should purify (her womb) with one menses. But a virgin need not purify." [2]

Prohibited Marriages of *Jāhiliyyah*

ʿĀ'ISHAH'S *ḤADĪTH*

ʿĀ'ishah (ﷺ) mentioned some forms of marriage that were common during *Jāhiliyyah* times. ʿUrwah Bin az-Zubayr (ﷺ) reported that ʿĀ'ishah (ﷺ) told him:

> "During *Jāhiliyyah*, marriage was of four different types:
>
> 1. The first was like the people's marriages today, whereupon a man would ask for another man's daughter or principal. He would give her a *ṣadāq*

---

1 Recorded by Abū Dāwūd, at-Tirmithī, and others. Verified to be authentic by al-Albānī (*Ṣaḥīḥ ul-Jāmiʿ* no. 6507, 6508 & *Irwā'ul-Ghalīl* no. 2137).

2 Recorded by al-Bukhārī (without *isnād*) and al-Bayhaqī from Nāfiʿ. Verified to be authentic by al-Albānī (*Irwā'ul-Ghalīl* no. 2139).

and marry her.

2. The second was that a man would tell his wife after she is clean from menses, 'Invite so and so, and get impregnated by him.' Thus her husband would stay away from her and avoid touching her until it became clear if she was pregnant from that man. Once she was definitely pregnant, her husband may have intercourse with her if he wished. They only did that seeking a noble descent for the child.

3. The third was that a group of men, less than ten in total, would all go to a woman and perform intercourse with her. If she became pregnant, she would wait until she delivered the child. A few nights later, she would summon all of them, and none of them may refuse to go to her. When they had arrived, she would say, 'You know what you have done; and I have given birth, so this child is yours, O so-and-so.' Thus she names whomever she wishes of them, and that man may not refuse annexing that child to him.

4. The fourth was that a large number of men would go to one woman, and she would not reject anyone who came to her. Those were the prostitutes who raised over their doors flags as signs for those who wished to go to them. And if one of them became pregnant, she would wait until she delivered, summon all the men who had intercourse with her, and have those who specialized in detecting likenesses determine the man whom the child resembled the most so as to append it to him; and he would not have the option to refuse that.

So after Muḥammad (ﷺ) came with the Truth, he revoked all forms of marriage of *Jāhiliyyah* — except for the marriage of the people today." [1]

The second, third, and fourth forms of marriage mentioned in this *ḥadīth* are all clearly prohibited, and will be briefly discussed below.

Partially Open Marriage

This is the second type in the above *ḥadīth*. A man would urge his wife to have intercourse with another man who is distinguished with courage, nobleness, etc. His purpose is to have her bear a child carrying some noble qualities from that man. Needless to say, this is outright *zinā*, and a man who does it is clearly a *dayyūth*.

Marriage of a Group

This is the third type in the above *ḥadīth*. A number of men would all be married to the same woman and simultaneously have intercourse with her. That represents a clear degeneracy and deviation from the pure human nature and values. It further shows how disgraced and despised women were before *Islām*.

Public Prostitution

The fourth type in the above *ḥadīth* is a form of public prostitution. A woman would have a clear sign on her house indicating that she welcomes any man who wishes to have her for a brief period of time, in exchange for an agreed pay. Unfortunately, that kind of multiple "marriage" or "profession" is still practiced in most of the so-called "civilized" nations of our time.

Other Prohibited Marriages

There are other forms of marriage that were practiced during *Jāhiliyyah* or the early years of *Islām*, but were subsequently prohibited. Among them are the following.

---

1 Recorded by al-Bukhārī and Abū Dāwūd.

Marriage of *Mutah*

The *mutʿah* (enjoyment) marriage is a temporary marriage. Its duration is specified at the time that the contract is executed. At the end of the term, the two spouses leave each other without divorce. Furthermore, the two partners do not inherit from each other.

This type of marriage was common during *Jāhiliyyah*. Its purpose was to merely fulfill a physical need for the man. Allāh's Messenger (ﷺ) permitted it for some time, but ended up prohibiting it permanently.

Abū Hurayrah (ﷺ) reported that Allāh's Messenger (ﷺ) said:

«هدمَ المُتعةَ النّكاحُ والطلاقُ والعدّةُ والميراثُ.»

‹*Mutʿah* has been abolished by marriage, divorce, *ʿiddah*, and inheritance.› [1]

The *ʿulamā* differ as to whether the *mutʿah* marriage was prohibited during the fight of Khaybar or the Conquest of Makkah. The latter position appears to be stronger, and is adopted by most of the *ʿulamā*.

Sabrah Bin Maʿbid (ﷺ) reported that at the time of the Conquest of Makkah, Allāh's Messenger (ﷺ) said:

«يا أيها الناس! إني قد كنتُ أذِنتُ لكم في الاستمتاعِ من النساء، وإن اللّـهَ قد حرّم ذلك من يومِكم هذا إلى يوم القيامة. فمن كان عنده منهُنّ شيءٌ فليخل سبيلَه، ولا تأخذوا مما آتيتُموهنّ شيئاً.»

‹O people! I had previously permitted you to have women by way of *mutʿah*. But indeed, Allāh has now prohibited that until the Day of Resurrection. Thus, anyone who has any such women should let them go, and do not take any of what you gave them.› [2]

---

1 Recorded by Ibn Ḥibbān, ad-Dāraquṭnī, and al-Bayhaqī. Verified to be *ḥasan* by al-Albānī (*Ṣaḥīḥ ul-Jāmiʿ* no. 7022 & *aṣ-Ṣaḥīḥah* no. 2402).

2 Recorded by Muslim and Ibn Mājah.

Sabrah (📿) also reported:

> "On the year of the Conquest, Allāh's Messenger (📿)
> permitted us to enjoy women (with *mutʿah*) as we were
> entering Makkah. But he later prohibited it for us —
> even before we left Makkah." [1]

Ibn ʿAbbās (📿) did not know that Allāh's Messenger (📿)
prohibited the *mutʿah* marriage, so ʿAlī (📿) reproached him and said
to him:

> "Indeed, Allāh's Messenger (📿) prohibited enjoying
> women (*mutʿah*) on the day of Khaybar, and he
> prohibited eating the ordinary donkeys (contrary to
> zebras)." [2]

MARRIAGE OF *TAHLĪL*

If a man divorces his wife three times, he may not take her back unless
she first marries another man [3]. If the second husband divorces her, she
may then marry the first husband.

The woman must have intercourse with the second husband before
she becomes permissible to the first husband (if the second husband
willingly divorces her).

Ibn ʿUmar (📿) reported that a case was presented to Allāh's
Messenger (📿) as follows, "A man divorced his wife three times.
Another man then married her, closed the doors, and dropped the
curtains (i.e., he had full privacy with her), but divorced her without
performing intercourse with her. Would that make her permissible to
the first husband?" He (📿) replied:

$$\text{«لا تَحِلُّ للأول حتى يجامعها الآخر.»}$$

‹She does not become permissible for the first

---

1   Recorded by Muslim, Aḥmad, and al-Bayhaqī.
2   Recorded by al-Bukhārī, Muslim, and others.
3   Check *al-Baqarah* 2:229.

(husband) until the second performs intercourse with her.› [1]

Similarly, ʿĀʾishah, Anas, and ʿUbayd Ullāh Bin ʿAbbās (ﷺ) reported that Rufāʿah al-Qarẓī divorced his wife three times, after which she married ʿAbd ur-Raḥmān Bin az-Zubayr. But she did not allow him to approach her and came to the Prophet (ﷺ) claiming that he was impotent and requesting divorce. ʿAbd ur-Raḥmān refuted that saying that she actually wanted to go back to her first husband. Allāh's Messenger (ﷺ) then told her that that may not happen unless she had intercourse with the second husband. [2]

In order to overcome this restriction, some people apply a trick to make it possible for the woman to go back to her husband. Another man (called *muḥill* or *muḥallil*) would marry her, and include a condition in the marriage contract that, as soon as he copulates with her, their marriage becomes terminated. This is a form of *mutʿah* marriage, because it includes the temporary factor. In addition, it represents a clear defiance to Allāh's commands and instructions. Because of this, it deserved Allāh's curse.

ʿAlī Bin Abī Ṭālib, ʿAbdullāh Bin Masʿūd, and Jābir Bin ʿAbdillāh (ﷺ) reported that Allāh's Messenger (ﷺ) said:

«لعن اللّهُ المُحلِّلَ والمحَلَّلَ له.»

‹Allāh curses the one who performs *taḥlīl*, and the one for whom it is performed.› [3]

ʿUqbah Bin ʿĀmir (ﷺ) reported that Allāh's Messenger (ﷺ) said:

«ألا أخبركم بالتيس المستعار؟ هو المُحِلُّ، فلعن اللّهُ المُحلَّ والمحَلَّلَ له.»

---

1 Recorded by an-Nasāʾī, Aḥmad, and others. Verified to be authentic by al-Albānī (*Ṣaḥīḥ ul-Jāmiʿ* no. 7253 & *Irwāʾ ul-Ghalīl* no. 1887).

2 Recorded by al-Bukhārī, Muslim, and others. Review *Irwāʾ ul-Ghalīl* no. 1997 for the various reports of this *ḥadīth*.

3 Recorded by Aḥmad, an-Nasāʾī, and others. Verified to be authentic by al-Albānī (*Irwāʾ ul-Ghalīl* no. 1897 & *Ṣaḥīḥ ul-Jāmiʿ* no. 5101).

‹Shouldn't I tell you about the borrowed billy goat? It is a person who performs *taḥlīl*. May Allāh curse the one who performs *taḥlīl*, and the one for whom it is performed.› [1]

Nāfi' reported that a man said to Ibn 'Umar (⬥), "Is it permissible for me to marry a woman to make her lawful for her (previous) husband, even though he did not ask me to do it, and I did it without his knowledge." He replied:

"No! The marriage should only be based on real interest: if you like her you keep her, and if you dislike her you divorce her. We indeed used to consider this (*taḥlīl*) as *zinā* during Allāh's Messenger's (⬥) time. And those who do it will continue to be in a state of *zinā*, if his intention was to make her lawful to the other man, even if they stay together for twenty years!" [2]

MARRIAGE OF *SHIGHĀR*

Shighār is a process whereby two men inter-marry each others' daughters or principals without either one taking a *mahr*. Thus, they consider their inter-marriage as the due *mahr*s. Nāfi' (⬥) explained:

"*Shighār* is that a man would marry his daughter to another man with the condition that the other man would marry him his daughter. And they would not require any *mahr* in between them." [3]

Ibn 'Umar (⬥) reported that Allāh's Messenger (⬥) prohibited *shighār* marriages [4] and said:

---

1   Recorded by Ibn Mājah, al-Ḥakim, and al-Bayhaqī. Verified to be *hasan* by al-Albānī (*Ṣaḥīḥ ul-Jāmi'* no. 2596 & *Irwā' ul-Ghalīl* no. 1897).

2   Recorded by al-Ḥākim, al-Bayhaqī, and aṭ-Ṭabarānī. Verified to be authentic by al-Albānī (*Irwā' ul-Ghalīl* no. 1898).

3   Recorded by al-Bukhārī, Muslim, and others.

4   Recorded by al-Bukhārī, Muslim, and others.

«لا شِغارَ في الإسلامِ.»

‹No *shighār* (is permissible) in *Islām*.› [1]

Even when dowries are specified, this inter-marriage remains as a source of doubt that should be avoided.

Al-Aʿraj reported that al-ʿAbbās Bin ʿAbdillāh Bin ʿAbbās gave his daughter in marriage to ʿAbd ur-Raḥmān Bin al-Ḥakam, and ʿAbd ur-Raḥmān gave his daughter to him in marriage, and they named some *mahr*s. Yet, Muʿāwiyah (who was the *khalīfah* then) wrote to Marwān Bin al-Ḥakam commanding him to separate between them and saying:

> "This is the *shighār* marriage that Allāh's Messenger (ﷺ) prohibited." [2]

Marriage with the Intention of Divorce

Some men may marry a woman for a specific purpose, intending within themselves to divorce her as soon as that purpose is accomplished. An example of this is a common practice in some Western countries of a foreigner marrying a native woman in order to obtain residency in her country, and planning to divorce her as soon as he achieves that.

If the marriage contract sets a term for this kind of marriage, it becomes a prohibited form of *mutʿah* marriage. If it does not, the majority of the scholars consider this marriage valid, but consider the man sinful because he deceives the woman by hiding her initial intention from her.

---

1 Recorded by Muslim and others.

2 Recorded by Aḥmad, Abū Dāwūd, and Ibn Ḥibbān. Verified to be *ḥasan* by al-Albānī (*Irwā'ul-Ghalīl* no. 1896).

Marrying Non-Muslims

General Rule

Allāh (ﷻ) prohibited marriage with the *mushriks*, males and females:

﴿وَلَا تَنكِحُوا۟ ٱلْمُشْرِكَٰتِ حَتَّىٰ يُؤْمِنَّ، وَلَأَمَةٌ مُّؤْمِنَةٌ خَيْرٌ مِّن مُّشْرِكَةٍ
وَلَوْ أَعْجَبَتْكُمْ. وَلَا تُنكِحُوا۟ ٱلْمُشْرِكِينَ حَتَّىٰ يُؤْمِنُوا۟، وَلَعَبْدٌ مُّؤْمِنٌ
خَيْرٌ مِّن مُّشْرِكٍ وَلَوْ أَعْجَبَكُمْ. أُو۟لَٰٓئِكَ يَدْعُونَ إِلَى ٱلنَّارِ، وَٱللَّهُ
يَدْعُوٓا۟ إِلَى ٱلْجَنَّةِ وَٱلْمَغْفِرَةِ بِإِذْنِهِۦ﴾ البقرة ٢٢١

«And do not marry pagan women until they believe (in Allāh alone). Indeed, a believing female slave (of Allāh) is better than a pagan, even though she (the pagan) might appeal to you. And do not marry pagan men until they believe. Indeed, a believing male slave (of Allāh) is better than a pagan, even though he might appeal to you. Those (*mushriks*) invite (you) to the Fire, whereas Allāh invites to *Jannah* and to forgiveness, by His permission.» [1]

Every non-Muslim is a *mushrik*. This includes the People of the Scripture (the Jews and Christians) if they worship anyone besides Allāh (like Jesus or ʿUzayr) or hold other wrong beliefs about Allāh (ﷻ).

Exception to the Rule

Allāh (ﷻ) made exception to the above rule by permitting Muslim men to marry Jewish and Christian women — with an important condition: they must be chaste, which means that they are not promiscuous and have not previously had illegitimate sexual relationships with men. Allāh (ﷻ) says:

---

1 *Al-Baqarah* 2:221.

﴿ٱلْيَوْمَ أُحِلَّ لَكُمُ ٱلطَّيِّبَٰتُ، وَطَعَامُ ٱلَّذِينَ أُوتُوا۟ ٱلْكِتَٰبَ حِلٌّ لَّكُمْ،
وَطَعَامُكُمْ حِلٌّ لَّهُمْ، وَٱلْمُحْصَنَٰتُ مِنَ ٱلْمُؤْمِنَٰتِ، وَٱلْمُحْصَنَٰتُ
مِنَ ٱلَّذِينَ أُوتُوا۟ ٱلْكِتَٰبَ مِن قَبْلِكُمْ، إِذَآ ءَاتَيْتُمُوهُنَّ أُجُورَهُنَّ،
مُحْصِنِينَ غَيْرَ مُسَٰفِحِينَ وَلَا مُتَّخِذِي أَخْدَانٍ، وَمَن يَكْفُرْ بِٱلْإِيمَٰنِ
فَقَدْ حَبِطَ عَمَلُهُ وَهُوَ فِي ٱلْءَاخِرَةِ مِنَ ٱلْخَٰسِرِينَ ۝﴾ المائدة ٥

«This day all good foods have been made lawful for
you; and the food of those who have been given the
Scripture is lawful for you, and your food is lawful
for them; and (lawful for you for marriage are)
chaste believing women and chaste women from
among those who were given the Scripture before
you — when you have given them their due
compensation — desiring by that chastity, not illicit
relationship or taking secret lovers. And whoever
denies the faith — his deeds have surely become
worthless, and he will be, in the Hereafter, among
the losers.» [1]

WHO "THE PEOPLE OF THE BOOK" ARE

Some of the companions took the position that the above permission
only applied to the "unitarian" People of the Book. They argued in
regard to a trinitarian Christian woman, "What form of *shirk* is worse
than her claim that her Lord is Jesus?" For example, 'Alī (﷜) said:

> "The Arab Christians' slaughtering may not be eaten,
> because they do not hold to the (true) Christianity
> except by drinking alcohol." [2]

On the other hand, 'Umar (﷜) was asked whether it was lawful to

---

1   *Al-Māʾidah* 5:5.

2   Recorded by 'Abd ur-Razzāk and al-Bayhaqī. Verified to be authentic by
     Muṣṭafā al-'Adawī (*Jāmiʿu Aḥkām in-Nisāʾ* 3:125).

eat from the slaughtered meat of a group of Jews who read the Torah and observed the Sabbath but do not believe in resurrection. He said:

"They are a group from the People of the Book." [1]

Ibn ʿAbbās (ﷺ) said:

"Eat from the slaughtering of the Taghlib [2] and marry from their women." [3]

Az-Zuhrī (ﷺ) was asked about the slaughtering of the Arab Christians. He replied that they were lawful, and said:

"Whoever embraces a religion is considered one of its people." [4]

Ash-Shaʿbī (ﷺ) said in answer to a similar question:

"Allāh has made their slaughtering lawful, and your Lord is never forgetful." [5]

There are many other similar authentic reports from the *salaf* in which they consider the Christians and Jews as being from "the People of the Book" regardless of their beliefs. This appears to be the stronger of the two opinions. [6]

---

1   Recorded by ʿAbd ur-Razzāk and al-Bayhaqī. Verified to be authentic by Muṣṭafā al-ʿAdawī (*Jāmiʿu Aḥkām in-Nisāʾ* 3:126).

2   An Arab Christian tribe.

3   Recorded by Ibn Abī Shaybah. Verified to be authentic by Muṣṭafā al-Adawī (*Jāmiʿu Aḥkām in-Nisāʾ* 3:126).

4   Recorded by ʿAbd ur-Razzāk. Verified to be authentic by Muṣṭafā al-ʿAdawī (*Jāmiʿu Aḥkām in-Nisāʾ* 3:127).

5   Recorded by ʿAbd ur-Razzāk. Verified to be authentic by Muṣṭafā al-ʿAdawī (*Jāmiʿu Aḥkām in-Nisāʾ* 3:127).

6   Review *Jāmiʿu Aḥkām in-Nisāʾ* 3:122-128.

A Hard-to-fulfill Condition

The condition of "chastity" does not usually hold in our time. A chaste woman is one who has been preserved within her house like a jewel, never being involved in kissing, touching, petting, or any form of promiscuous relationships with men other than her husband.

A non-Muslim woman has no faith that would prevent her from committing the sin. Added to that is today's open Western culture that has permitted *zinā* with the approval and encouragement of the parents and relatives. It is seldom to find a girl passing her teenage years without being previously involved in sexual relationships. Virginity is now a hard-to-find rarity among the Westerners.

Some people may ask, "What if a Christian woman repented from her former promiscuous behavior? Would it then be permissible to marry her?" The answer is that repentance is an act of worship specific to the Muslims. Its first condition is *ikhlāṣ* (sincerity) to Allāh. How could a non-Muslim fulfill this? Her only repentance, then, is by embracing *Islām* (for the sake of Allāh, and not for marriage).

Even at the peak of the *Islām*ic power and dominance, ʿUmar (ﷺ) was against marrying from the People of the Book. Abū Wāʾil reported that Huthayfah (ﷺ) married a Jewish woman. ʿUmar (ﷺ) wrote to him, "Divorce her." He wrote back, "If this is unlawful, I will divorce her." ʿUmar (ﷺ) wrote:

"إني لا أزعم أنها حرام، ولكني أخاف أن تعاطوا المومسات منهن."

> "I do not claim that it is unlawful, but I fear that you (Muslims) will soon partake of their whores (if everyone takes this matter lightly)." [1]

Jābir (ﷺ) was asked about marrying Jewish and Christian women. He replied:

> "We used to marry them during the times of fighting when we were with Saʿd Bin Abī Waqqāṣ in al-Kūfah.

---

1 Recorded by al-Bayhaqī and Saʿīd Bin Manṣūr. Verified to be authentic by Muṣtafā al-ʿAdawī (*Jāmiʿu Aḥkām in-Nisāʾ* 3:122).

> That was because we could then hardly find any Muslim women. But when we came back (from the fights), we divorced them." [1]

CONCLUSION

In our times, the Muslims are weak and have the lower hand, even in their own countries. If one marries a non-Muslim woman, he will not be able to enforce an *Islām*ic environment in his own house. He will see her wear and worship the cross, pray to Jesus, eat pork, and raise his children upon disbelief. This, by itself, is a major act of disobedience that he would bring about for himself and his own offspring. What sin is greater than this sin? This alone is a sufficient reason for the prohibition of such marriages under the current circumstances.

The excuse that some people give, "This marriage is better than committing *zinā*,," is absurd. First, such a marriage is not permissible to start with. Second, its outcome is worse than the worst outcome of *zinā*.

Therefore, young men should fear Allāh and only marry Muslim women who will be good companions for them in this life and would help raise their children upon *Islām*.

---

1 Recorded by ash-Shāfiʿī (in *al-Umm*) and al-Bayhaqī. Verified to be authentic by Muṣṭafā al-ʿAdawī (*Jāmiʿu Aḥkām in-Nisāʾ* 3:124).

APPENDIX

The following sample marriage certificate was developed by the author — as a result of numerous marriages that he performed over more than twenty years. It incorporates the *Sunnah* requirements for a marriage, as well as the legal requirements for Muslims living in the United States or other Western countries.

Note that the spacing and column-widths have greatly been reduced to allow the certificate to fit on the paper-size of this book. One is advised to modify that as needed when making an enlarged version.

بسم الله الرحمن الرحيم

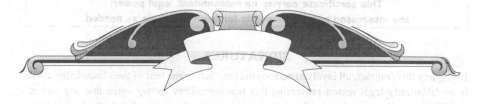

ISLĀMIC MARRIAGE CERTIFICATE

PERSONAL DATA

	Bride	Groom
Full Name		
Address and Phone Number		
Birth Place & Date		
Proof of Identity		
Father's Name		
Mother's (Maiden) Name		
Representative (*Walī*), His Address and Phone Number		(optional)

MARRIAGE DATA

Legal Marriage	State or Locality	Record Number	Date
***Islām*ic Marriage**	Location		Date
***Ṣadāq* (dowry for the bride)**			
Terms & Conditions (optional)			

This is to certify that, on this day, the bride's and the groom's parties have exchanged the *ījāb* and *qabūl* (offering and acceptance), in accordance with the Allāh's (ﷻ) Book and His Messenger Muḥammad's (ﷺ) Guidance. Finding no apparent *Islām*ic obstacle to prevent this marriage, I therefore pronounce the above-named groom and bride are husband and wife.

This certificate carries no independent legal power;
the interested parties must file for legal marriage as needed.

SIGNATURES

By signing this contract, all involved persons declare that, to the best of their knowledge, there is no *Islām*ically legal reason preventing this marriage. They further agree that any and all possible future disputes related to this marriage must be resolved according to the *Islām*ic Law.

Bride	*Wali*	Bridegroom

Witness 1, address, phone no.	Witness 2, address, phone no.	Officiant (*Imam* or Judge)

Serial Number	Recording Date

SEAL

REFERENCES

Ādāb uz-Zifāfi fis-Sunnat il-Muṭahharah (The Etiquettes of Wedding According to the Purified *Sunnah*), New Edition, Muḥammad Nāṣir ud-Dīn al-Albānī, al-Maktabat ul-Islāmiyyah, Amman, 1414 (1994).

Aḥādīth ul-Radā — Ḥujjiyyatuhā wa-Fiqhuhā (The *Ḥadīths* Concerning Breast-Feeding — their Authority and Understanding), Saʿd al-Marṣifī, Muʾassasat ur-Rayyān, Beirut, 1415 (1994).

Aḥādīth ul-Wilāyati fin-Nikāḥ (The *Ḥadīths* Concerning Guardianship in Marriage), Saʿd al-Marṣifī, Muʾassasat ur-Rayyān, Beirut, 1418 (1997).

Aḥkām uz-Zawāji fī Ḍawʾ il-Kitābi was-Sunnah (Marriage Regulations in Light of the Book and *Sunnah*), ʿUmar Sulaymān al-Ashqar, Dār un-Nafāʾis, Amman, 1418 (1997).

Al-Ḥayāt uz-Zawjiyyat us-Saʿīdah fī Ẓill il-Islām (The Happy Life of Marriage in the Light of *Islām*), ʿAbd ul-Ḥamīd Khazzār, Dār ul-Furqān, Amman, 1410 (1990).

Al-Ifṣāḥ ʿan Aḥādīth in-Nikāḥ (Declaration of the *Ḥadīths* Concerning Marriage), Ibn Ḥajar al-Haythamī, Dār ʿAmmār, Amman, 1406 (1986).

Al-Jāmiʿu li-Aḥkām il-Qurʾān (The Collective Reference in Regard to the *Qurʾān*ic Rulings), al-Qurṭubī, Dār ul-Fikr, Beirut.

Al-Mufaṣṣal fI Aḥkām il-Marʾah (The Detailed Book in Regard to the Regulations for the Woman), Vol. 6, ʿAbd ul-Karīm Zaydān, Muʾassasat ur-Risālah, Beirut, 1417 (1997).

Asrār uz-Zawāj is-Saʿīd (Secrets for a Happy Marriage), Buthaynah al-ʿIrāqī, Dār uṭ Ṭuwayq, Riyadh, 1417 (1997).

Az-Zawāju fī Ẓill il-Islām (Marriage in the Shade of *Islām*), ʿAbd ur-Raḥmān ʿAbd ul-Khāliq, ad-Dār us-Salafiyyah, Kuwait, 1408 (1988).

Az-Zinā, Aḥkāmuhū, Asbābuhū, Natāʾijuhū, wal-Wiqāyatu Minh (*Zinā*, Its Regulations, Causes, Results, and Protection against It), Jabr Maḥmūd al-Fuḍaylāt, Dār ʿAmmār, Amman, 1410 (1989).

Fatāwā wa-Rasāʾil lin-Nisāʾ, Muḥammad Bin Ṣāliḥ al-ʿUthaymīn, Maktabat Shams, Riyadh, 1410 (1990).

Fiqh ul-Usrah (Regulations of the Family), Aḥmad ʿAlī Ṭāhā Rayyān, the American Open University, Virginia, USA.

Fiqh uz-Zawāj (Regulations of Marriage), Ṣāliḥ Bin Ghānim as-Sadlān, Dār Balansiyah, Riyadh, 1416 (1996).

Fatḥ ul-Bārī Sharḥ Ṣāḥīḥ il-Bukhārī (The Creator's Help in the Explanation of *Ṣaḥīḥ ul-Bukhārī*), al-Ḥāfiẓ Ibn Ḥajar al-ʿAsqalānī, Dār ul-Kutub il-ʿIlmiyyah, Beirut, 1989.

Handbook of Marriage in Islam, Second Edition, Abdullah Muhammad Khouj, Islamic Center of Washington, D.C., Washington, D.C., 1992.

Ḥuqūq ul-Marʾat il-Muslimah fil-Qurʾāni was-Sunnah (The Rights of the Muslim Woman in the *Qurʾān* and *Sunnah*), Muḥammad Furayjah, al-Maktab ul-Islāmī, Beirut, 1416 (1996).

Ḥuqūq un-Nisāʾ fil-Islām (The Rights of Women in *Islām*), Muḥammad Rashīd Riḍā & Muḥammad Nāṣir ud-Dīn al-Albānī, al-Maktab ul-Islāmī, Beirut, 1404 (1984).

Ḥuqūq uz-Zawjayn (The Rights of the Two Spouses), Abū al-Aʿlā al-Mawdūdī, ad-Dār us-Saʿūdiyyah, Jeddah, 1405 (1985).

Irwāʾ ul-Ghalīli fī Takhrīji Aḥādīthi Manār is-Sabīl (Quenching the Thirst in Researching the *Ḥadīth*s of *Manār us-Sabīl*), Muḥammad Nāṣir ud-Dīn al-Albānī, al-Maktab ul-Islāmī, Beirut, 1405 (1985).

Jāmiʿu Aḥkām in-Nisāʾ (The Collection of Rulings for Women), Vols. 3 & 5, Muṣṭafā al-ʿAdawī, Dār Ibn ʿAffān, Cairo, 1419 (1999).

Lin-Nisāʾi faqat, az-Zawjat uṣ-Ṣāliḥah (For Women Only: the Righteous Wife), Majdī Fatḥī as-Sayyid, Dār ur-Rāyah, Riyadh, 1414 (1993).

Munkarāt ul-Afrāḥ (Improper Acts During Celebrations), Maḥmūd Mahdī Istanbūlī (Editor), al-Maktab ul-Islāmī, Beirut, 1405 (1985).

Rawḍat ul-Muḥibbīn wa-Nuzhat ul-Mushtāqīn, Ibn Qayyim il-Jawziyyah, Dār ul-Kutub al-ʿIlmiyyah, Beirut, 1415 (1995).

Righteous Wife, the, Muhammad Shūmān, al-Hidaayah Publishing, Birmingham, 1417 (1996).

Sharḥu Qānūn il-Aḥwāl ish-Shakhṣiyyah (Explanation of the Law of Personal Affairs), Muṣtafā as-Sibāʿī, al-Maktab ul-Islāmī, Beirut, 1417 (1997).

Sharḥ us-Sunnah, al-Baghawī, Vol. 9, al-Maktab ul-Islāmī, Beirut, 1403 (1983).

Silsilat ul-Aḥādīth iṣ-Ṣaḥiḥah (The Series of Authentic *ḥadīth*s), Volumes 1 to 6, Muḥammad Nāṣir ud-Dīn al-Albānī, Maktabat ul-Maʿārif, Riyadh, 1415 to 1417 (1995 to 1996).

Taḥthīru Wulāt il-Umūr min al-Mughālāti fil-Muhūr (Warning the Guardians Against Excessiveness in Dowries), Muḥammad Mūsā al-Bayḍānī, at-Tawʿiyah al-Islāmiyyah, Egypt, 1408 (1988).

Tuḥfat ul-ʿArūs (The Gift to the Brides), Maḥmūd Mahdī Istanbūlī, al-Maktab ul-Islāmī, Beirut, 1407 (1986).

Uṣūl ul-Muʿāsharat iz-Zawjiyyah (Fundamentals of the Marital Relationship), Muḥammad Kanʿān, Dār ul-Bashāʾir, Beirut, 1419 (1999).

Usus Ukhtiyār iz-Zawjayni fil-Kitābi was-Sunnah (The Fundamentals for Selection of the Two Spouses in the Book and *Sunnah*), Muṣṭafā aṣ-Ṣayāṣinah, Dār ur-Rāyah, Riyadh, 1408 (1988).

Zād ul-Maʿād Fī Hadyi Khayr il-ʿIbād (Provision for the Hereafter from the Guidance of the Best of People), Ibn Qayyim il-Jawziyyah, Muʾassasat ur-Rayyān, Beirut, 1418 (1998).

ʿIshrat un-Nisāʾ (Treatment of Women), Aḥmad Bin Shuʿayb an-Nasāʾī, Muʾassasat ul-Kutub ith-Thaqāfiyyah, Beirut, 1409 (1989).

ʿIshrat un-Nisāʾ min al-Alif ilal-Yāʾ (Treatment of Women from A to Z), Usāmah ʿAbdurrazzāq, Dār ul-Waṭan, Riyadh, 1419 (1998).

ARABIC TERMS

A number of Arabic terms are frequently used in *Islām*ic discussions, and seem to constitute a basic vocabulary that needs to be available to the readers of most books on *Islām*. We attempt to provide such terms, together with their definitions, in the following "Glossary" section. Other terms pertinent to the current book are included in the "Index" section, together with a page-reference indicating where they are defined in this book.

A: Glossary of Common Terms

Term	**Definition**
Adab	Good characters or manners; etiquettes. Plural: *Ādāb*.
Al-Fātiḥah	The first chapter of the *Qur'ān*.
Āmīn	Means, "O Allāh, answer my supplication."
Anṣār	"The Supporters": the residents of al-Madīnah who supported the Prophet (ﷺ) and the *Muhājirūn*.
A<u>th</u>ān	Call to the prayer.
Āyah	A *Qur'ān*ic phrase approximately equal to one sentence, but sometimes longer or shorter than that; plural: *āyāt*.
Āyāt	Plural of *āyah*.
Bid'ah	Innovation in the creed or in acts of worship.
Da'wah	Call or mission.
Dīn	Religion. It is usually used in reference to the religion of *Islām*.

Term	Definition
Dīnār	A valuable old currency that was made of gold.
Dirham	A low-value old currency that was made of silver or copper.
Du'ā'	Supplication.
Fajr	Dawn. It usually applies to the first daily obligatory prayer, whose time extends from dawn until sunrise.
Farḍ	Obligation.
Farḍ Kifāyah	A communal obligation; if some Muslims perform it, the obligation is considered fulfilled by all; and if none does, all Muslims are considered sinful.
Farḍ 'Ayn	An individual obligation, i.e., an obligation that each individual must fulfill.
Fatwā	A religious verdict; plural: *fatāwā* or *fatāwī*.
Fiqh	The ability to understand and derive conclusions from the available evidence. It is often applied to the subject of "*Islām*ic jurisprudence" that deals with the practical regulations in *Islām*.
Fitnah	Trial, test, temptation, or affliction.
Ghayb	The world beyond our senses or perception.
Ghusl	A ritual bath required after intercourse, ejaculation, or after a women becomes clean from her menses.
Ḥadīth	Reports of the Prophet's sayings, actions, and approvals. We use *ḥadīth* (plural *ḥadīth*s) to indicate individual report(s), and *Ḥadīth* with upper case Ḥ to indicate the subject of *Ḥadīth* specialty.
Ḥajj	Pilgrimage to Makkah.
Ḥalāl	Permissible.

Term	**Definition**
Ḥalqah	A circle or ring. It normally refers to a study circle.
Ḥarām	Prohibited.
Ḥasan	Good or acceptable. This is usually mentioned when indicating the degree of authenticity of some reports.
Ḥijāb	Cover. It usually refers to a woman's clothing that covers all of her body except her face and hands.
Hijrah	Migration. It usually refers to migration from Makkah to al-Madīnah.
Ijmāʿ	Consensus of the scholars.
Ijtihād	Exerting *juhd* (maximum possible effort) to reach the right conclusion based on the available evidence.
Imām	A leader or distinguished *Islām*ic scholar. It is often applied to the leader of prayer.
Īmān	Belief or conviction.
Isnād	Chain of narrators of a *ḥadīth*.
Jāhiliyyah	The era of extreme ignorance (*jahl*) and disbelief that preceded the advent of the Prophet Muḥammad (ﷺ).
Jamāʿah	A Muslim congregation or gathering. It is often applied to the congregational prayers. *Al-Jamāʿah* (the *Jamāʿah*) refers to the original community of the *ṣaḥābah* and their true followers through the ages.
Janāzah	A funeral or a deceased's prepared body.
Jannah	The gardens of paradise.
Jihād	Striving or fighting for Allāh's cause.

Term	Definition
Jinn	An indivisible creation that Allāh created from fire and smoke, and to which belongs Satan. It is sometimes translated as "demons".
Jumuʿah	Friday. It also applies to the Friday prayer.
Kāfir	A person who practices *kufr*. Plural: "*kuffār*".
Khalīfah	Derives from *khalafa*, which means "succeeded" or "followed". It commonly refers to a Muslim ruler who succeeded the Prophet (ﷺ) in leading the *Muslim*s. Plural: *khulafāʾ*.
Khamr	Alcoholic beverages.
Khilāfah	Successorship. It usually refers to the period of rule of a *khalīfah*.
Kufr	Disbelief or rejection of faith.
Khuṭbah	Speech or sermon.
Maghrib	Sunset. It is usually applied to the fourth daily obligatory prayer, whose time extends from sunset until the red light disappears from the horizon.
Makrūh	An act that is disapproved in *Islām*.
Maḥram	A person who is closely related to another in such a way as to permanently prohibit them from marrying each other. This relationship results from blood, suckling, or marriage ties. A woman's *maḥram*s are: her father, grandfather, son, grandson, brother, immediate uncle (from the mother's or father's side), father in law, son in law, foster son, foster brother, etc. Examples of non-*maḥram*s: cousins (from both sides), step brothers, brothers in law, etc.
Masjid	A place designated for *sujūd*. It usually refers to a mosque.

Term	Definition
Ma<u>th</u>hab	Way or approach. It usually refers to one of the four *Islāmic* schools of *fiqh* established by the Four *Imāms*: Abū Ḥanīfah an-Nuʿmān Bin Thābit, Mālik Bin Anas, Muḥammad Bin Idrīs ash-Shāfiʿī, and Aḥmad Bin Ḥanbal — May Allāh bestow His mercy on them all.
Muhājir	A *ṣaḥābī* who made *Hijrah* from Makkah to al-Madīnah. Plural: *muhājirūn* or *muhājirīn.*
Mujāhid	A person who performs *jihād.* Plural: *mujāhidūn* or *mujāhidīn.*
Munkar	Disapproved; rejected.
Muṣallā	A place designated for *ṣalāh.* Most commonly, it applies to the grounds where the prayers of *ʿīd* and *janāzah* are performed.
Mushrik	See "*shirk*".
Nafl	Extra, voluntary, or supererogatory deeds.
Qadar	Allāh's decree and measure.
Qiblah	The direction of al-Kaʿbah in Makkah.
Qudusī	Holy. A *qudusī ḥadīth* is a *ḥadīth* that the Prophet (ﷺ) relates from his Lord (ﷻ).
Rakʿah	Means a full prayer unit, because it contains only one *rukūʿ*. Plural: *rakʿāt.*
Ramaḍān	The month of fasting. It is the ninth month of the *Islāmic* lunar calendar.
Rukūʿ	The act of bowing in the prayer. It derives from the verb *rakaʿa* which means "bowed down".
Ṣadaqah	Charity.
Ṣaḥābah	The Prophet's companions; singular: *ṣaḥābī.*

Term	Definition
Ṣaḥīḥ	True or authentic.
Salaf	The early righteous pioneers and scholars of *Islām*—the *ṣaḥābah* and their true followers.
Ṣalāh	The prayer.
Salām	Peace. It also means the greeting with peace (*as-salāmu ʿalaykum*) among the Muslims.
Sanad	Same as *isnād*.
Shahādah	Testimony; it is mostly applied to the testimony of *Islām*: "There is no true deity but Allāh, and Muḥammad is Allāh's Messenger." Also, it is often applied to the most truthful form of physical testimony, which is martyrdom in Allāh's (ﷻ) cause.
Shahīd	A person martyred for Allāh's cause. Feminine: *Shahīdah*.
Sharʿ	It deriving from *sharaʿa*, which means "legislated". It is usually used in reference to the *Islām*ic Law. *Sharʿī* means a legislated or permissible matter in *Islām*.
Sharīʿah	Same as "*sharʿ*".
Shaykh	Old man; learned man in *Islām*; teacher; narrator.
Shirk	Polytheism, ascribing divinity to other than Allāh, or joining partners with Him in worship. A pagan or a person who practices *shirk* is a *mushrik*.
Ṣiyām	Fasting.
Sujūd	The act of prostration in the prayer.
Sunnah	Way, guidance, teachings, etc.
Sūrah	*Qurʾān*ic chapter.

Term	**Definition**
Tābiʿī	A student of the *ṣaḥābah*. Singular: *tābiʿūn* or *tābiʿīn*.
Tafsīr	*Qurʾān*ic commentaries and interpretations.
Takbīr	Saying, "*Allāhu Akbar* — Allāh is the greatest."
Tahlīl	Saying, "*Lā ilāha illallāh* — There is no true god except Allāh."
Taqlīd	Imitation — especially without knowledge.
Taqwā	Fearing Allāh and revering him.
Tasbīḥ	Saying, "*Subḥān Allāh* — Exalted is Allāh."
Tashahhud	Pronouncing the *Shahādah*. It is mostly applied to the part of the prayer where one sits, pronounces the *Shahādah*, invokes *ṣalāh* upon the Messenger, and supplicates.
Taslīm	Saying *salām*, especially to conclude the prayer.
T͟hikr	Remembering Allāh and mentioning Him.
Ummah	Community, nation, or followers.
Wājib	Obligatory or required.
Witr	Odd numbered. The entire night prayer is sometimes called *witr* because the total number of its *rakʿāt* is odd.
Wuḍūʾ	Ablution for the prayer. It consists of rinsing the mouth, blowing the nose, washing the face, washing the forearms to the elbows, wiping over the head (including the ears), and washing the feet up to the ankles.
Zakāh	Obligatory charity.
Zinā	Adultery or fornication.

Term	Definition
Ẓuhr	Noon. It is usually applied to the second daily obligatory prayer, whose time extends from the sun's crossing the zenith until the time when the shadows are as long as the objects.
ʿAbd	Devoted servant and worshipper; plural: *ʿibād*.
ʿĀlim	A scholar or learned man; plural: *ʿulamāʾ*. *ʿAllāmah* is an exaggerated form of *ʿālim*.
ʿAṣr	After noon. It is usually applied to the third daily obligatory prayer, whose time extends from when the shadows are as long as the objects until sunset.
ʿIbād	See "*ʿabd*".
ʿĪd	A day of celebration in *Islām*. There are two annual *ʿīd*s (*al-fiṭr* and *al-Aḍḥā*) and one weekly *ʿīd* (the day of *Jumuʿah*).
ʿIshāʾ	Night. It is usually applied to the fifth and last daily obligatory prayer, whose time extends from the disappearance of the red light from the horizon until the middle of the night (which is half way between sunset and dawn).
ʿUlamāʾ	See "*ʿālim*".

B: Index